GREEK
Mythology
by Sophia Kokkinou

D0401460

GREEK
Mythology
by Sophia Kokkinou

COPYRIGHT © 1989
SOPHIA KOKKINOU
Rue, Aegeou Pelagous 47
153 42 Ag. Paraskevi
Athenes-GREECE
e-mail: kokkinos@otenet.gr
Tel.: 0030-210 6391710
fax: 0030-210 6005890

15th EDITION

EDITOR:
SOPHIA KOKKINOU

LAY OUT 1st EDITION:
MARIA PANTELI
PRINTED BY:
S. NANOS
PHOTOTYPESETTING:
FOTRON S.A.

BIBLIOGRAPHY:
Hesiod, The Theogony
Homer, The Iliad
Homer, The Odyssey
Pausanias, Description of Greece
Hamilton Edith, Mythology
Larousse, Encyclopedia of
Mythology, Pietman.
H.J. Rose, A Handbook of Greek
Mythology.
W.H.D. Rouse, Gods, Heroes, and
Men of Ancient Greece.
C.M. Bowra, Classical Greece
J. Rispen, Greek Mythology.
William Harlan Hale, The Horizon
Book of Ancient Greece.

CONTENTS

The three-bodied monster Nereus (Acropolis Museum)

THIS BOOKLET IS DEDICATED TO THE
ORDINARY VISITOR OF GREECE, TO THE
ONE WHO BRINGS ALONG KNOWLEDGE OF
THIS COUNTY'S CULTURE, BUT ALSO TO
THE ONE WHO DOES NOT KNOW, BUT
WANTS TO LEARN ABOUT THE IMMORTAL
GLORY THAT IS GREECE.

Bronze statue of Zeus, National Museum of Athens

Zeus and Cronos

INTRODUCTION

My purpose is to present the most important and interesting parts of Greek mythology.

The distinct characteristic of ancient Greek religion is its "anthropomorphism", that is the resemblance to mankind. The Greeks imagined their gods as human beings with the same passions and weaknesses. Gods fell in love, they were jealous, they hated, they had favorites among mortals. Sometimes they persecuted and sometimes they protected. Thus, they were always near man who tried to appease them with sacrifices and prayers. There was, however, a great difference between gods and humans: gods were "immortal and unchangeable through all time".

It is also important to notice that when Greek mythology was in its early formative stage, there were all these legendary monsters, dreadful demons and dragons. They were strong, using their strength only to destroy. As time passed and Zeus (Jupiter) became the chief of the Hellenic pantheon, nature calmed and order ruled. Zeus himself, at the beginning, was not the perfect god. Often he was cruel and savage. However, through the centuries, as the level of civilization rose, and by the time of Aeschylus (5th century B.C.), he became a high moral power. Thus, Zeus elevated mankind and helped it to reach the perfection of the classical period. Some of the gods' origin is not Greek, but as they passed to the Hellenic world from elsewhere, they became characteristically Greek.

Before examining each god in a separate chapter, we shall search for the primeval force of the whole story, because certainly, there must have been somebody who gave birth to the Olympian Gods. In Homer, the gods were already organized on the model of a Mycenean society, with Zeus as its ideal ruler. The earliest account of the beginning of things, is given by Hesiod.

Most of the names are given in Greek and Latin. A few obscure names are translated in parenthesis, helping you to understand their real meaning.

National Museum of Athens

SOURCES OF GREEK MYTHOLOGY

HOMER (8th century B.C.)   The greatest epic poet. The author of the Iliad and the Odyssey and probably of the 34 Homeric Hymns.

HESIOD (about 850 B.C.)   Author of the Theogony, a rich collection of religious lore.

PINDAR (518-438 B.C.)   The greatest lyric poet, author of the Odes.

AESCHYLUS (524-456 B.C.)   The great poetic dramatist, author of about 90 plays. He was the oldest of the Greek masters of tragedy (Aeschylus - Sophocles - Euripides).
Most of the plays of Aeschylus have have mythological subjects.

The Alexandrian poets (about 250 B.C.)   APOLLONIUS OF RHODES, THEOCRITUS and BION.

The writers   LUCIAN and APOLLODORUS

The Roman writers   VIRGIL, OVID and HORACE (HORATIUS)

PAUSANIAS (2nd century A.D.)   The famous Greek traveler, writer geographer. His "Description of Greece" is an important source of the history, topography and mythology of ancient Greece.

The discord of Poseidon and Athena over the ruling of the city of Athens.

PART I

THE
GREEK
GODS

Hesiod starts his Theogony:

"First Chaos (gaping void) came into being, next, the wide bosomed Gaea or Ge (earth) the eternal, and Eros (love) the most beautiful of the immortals..."

Chaos was the creative beginning, the starting point that contained the sperm of the universe. From Chaos, sprang Erebus (the nether world) and primeval Nichta (black night). From Erebus and Nichta were born Aither (the upper air sky) and Imera (day).

Immediately after Chaos, came Gaea, the Universal Mother. She in turn gave birth first to Ouranos or Uranus (heaven), then the Mountains and next Pontos (the sea). Then Gaea mated with Uranus and brought forth the first dynasty of the gods: the Titans, also called Uranides (descendants of Uranus). In addition, there were born the Cyclopes (round eyes) and the three Ekatoncheires (hundred hands).

1st DYNASTY URANUS - GAEA

12 TITANS 3 CYCLOPES
3 HECATONCHEIRES (Centimanus)

The TITANS, were six male and six female. The male Titans included Oceanus (the Ocean), Koios, Kreios, Hyperion, Japetos and Kronos or Cronus (Saturn in Latin). The Titanesses were Tethys, Theis, Themis, Mnemosyne, Phoebe and Rhea.

The CYCLOPES, were giants, with one eye in the middle of their forehead. Their names were Brontes (thunder man), Steropes (lightning man), and Argos (shiner).

The HECATONCHEIRES, were giants, with hundred hands and fifty heads. Their names were Kottys, Gyges and Briareos.

Uranus and Gaea produced offspring endlessly. Uranus, however, knew that one of his children would dethrone him, and threw them upon birth into the depths of the earth (Tartarus). Their mother Gaea, desperate over the loss of her children, arranged with her youngest son, the Titan Cronus, to take revenge on Uranus. Cronus, took a sickle and cut down his fathers genitals. Thus, Uranus lost his strength and Cronus became the new master.

Drops of the blood from Uranus' wound, gave birth to the fearful Erinyes and the Nymphes.

The immortal genitals, having been dropped into the sea, gathered foam about them and gave birth to Aphrodite (Venus), the goddess of love and beauty (see chapter Aphrodite).

Cronus, the great master, took his sister Rhea for wife. The couple ruled the Universe for aeons, and gave birth to the second dynasty of the gods, the so called Cronides (descendants of Cronus).

2nd DYNASTY CRONUS - RHEA

HESTIA (Vesta), **DEMETER** (Ceres), **HERA** (Juno), **HADES or PLUTO, POSEIDON** (Neptune), **ZEUS** (Jupiter)

But alas! The same drama started for Rhea, as did for her mother. Her husband Cronus, like his father, afraid of the prophecy, that he would be overthrown by one of his children, swallowed them. Helpless Rhea, following her mother's advice, offered her consort a stone wrapped in swaddling clothes instead of her last child. Cronus devoured the stone, thus saving the last baby-god, whose name was Zeus! Zeus found the third Dynasty of the gods, the dynasty of the Olympians. The new generation, led by Zeus rebelled against their monstrous parents, becoming the gods of a rationalistic and anthropomorphic religion of the Hellenic world, and later on of the Roman.

3rd DYNASTY THE OLYMPIC PANTHEON

ZEUS (Jupiter), **POSEIDON** (Neptune), **HADES OR PLUTO, HERA** (Juno)**DEMETER** (Ceres), **ATHENA** (Minerva), **APOLLO, ARTEMIS** (Diana), **HERMES** (Mercury), **ARES** (Mars), **APHRODITE** (Venus), **HEPHAESTOS** (Vulcan), **HESTIA** (Vesta), **DIONYSOS** (Bacchus), **PAN, ASKLEPIOS** (Aesculapius)

Mountain Olympus

OLYMPUS

It was natural for the Greeks to believe that the great gods had conquered the mighty rugged mountains which defied man. Mountain Olympus is the snow-capped mountain in Thessaly in northern Greece, standing 2.981 m. high (almost 10.000 feet), hiding the glorious palaces of the gods. There, they lived and cavorted and held council "in a climate of perpetual spring-time, on the very top, there is no wind or rain, the atmosphere is clear and the air fresh ..." (according to Odyssey Z' 41-46).
There, in this magnificence, one of the gods, Hephaestos, built all their palaces.

Bronze statue of Zeus, National Museum of Athens

ZEUS
(JUPITER)

Zeus was the father of gods and humans, the supreme ruler, the god of the natural celestial phenomena (rain, lightning, thunder). He was the one who controlled the fate of people; protector of justice, the god who watched over human beings; the perfect form of divinity and of morality perfection.

The epithets given to him by Homer and Hesiod are countless (numbering more than 150), and are typical of his many attributes. Zeus Xenios, Horkios, Nepheligeretis, Eunous, Iketes Saviour, Father, Lyceios and Olympios give the clues to the range of some of his responsibilities. His power was based on his supreme strength and wisdom. This supreme power was not unlimited though, as Fate was stronger. This fate is represented in Greek mythology by the goddesses of destiny; these were the three Moires* (three Fates), Clotho, Lachesis, Atropos. They were the fate of every man from birth till death. Gods were unable to oppose them, because fate was the law which governed the universe. This law though was made by Zeus. So we reach the conclusion of combining Zeus with Moires, and so he was called Moiragetis (the guide of Fates).

It is not an exaggeration to say that the Greeks gathered all the power and the perfection of the divine in himself. We see in him the first sperm of monotheism. His figure combined kindness, ethical superiority, wisdom, reason and justice. Zeus was the last son of Cronus and Rhea. We have seen that Cronus, afraid of the prophecy, that one of his

The three Moires, from a Roman relief.

* Moires (Fates): Clotho (the spinner), Lachesis (the apportioner), Atropos (the inflexible).

children was going to take his Kingdom away, devoured them immediately, just as they were born. We know how Rhea cheated him with the swaddled stone, so to protect her last child, brought Zeus to the island of Crete, and hid him in a cave on mountain Ida (Dicte).

The Couretes* and the Nymphs* undertook to bring up Zeus. The goat Amaltheia offered him her milk. The baby grew up in a few days and he became handsome and strong. He was ready now to face his father Cronus. When they met, Zeus explained who he was and forced his father to drink a special kind of tea, made with boiled emetic herb. This caused him to vomit. So, out of his stomach came first the swaddled stone and then the five children that he had devoured: Poseidon, Hera, Hades, Hestia and Demeter.

TITANOMACHIA
(The battle against the Titans)

Zeus became now a strong god, but he still had a lot of difficulties to overcome. So, he with his brothers and sisters undertook a fearful battle against Cronus and the Titans. (see page 13, first Dynasty) Zeus asked also the help of some Titans, who had been dropped by offered Zeus the lightning and the thunderbolt.

Zeus gave freedom also to the Hecatoncheires, the giants with hundred hands, and in exchange they offered him their great help.

This furious battle lasted ten years.

Zeus against the Titans

Cronus into Tartarus*.

Among them were the Cyclops, who were so happy to be free, that apart from their great help in this battle, they

---

* Couretes: Demons of vegetation and fertility.
* Nymphs: Lovely female spirits, not as important as the goddesses, but still divine. They were the guardians of things in nature and they lived in fountains, trees, rivers and mountains.
* Tartarus: Representation of the dark depths of the earth.

"A dreadful sound troubled the boundless sea.
The whole earth uttered a great cry.
Wide heaven, shaken groaned.
From its foundation far Olympus reeled beneath the onrush of the deathless gods, and trembling seized upon black Tartarus"

Zeus and the Olympians won and he finally became the only master on Mount Olympus.

GIGANTOMACHY
(The battle against the Giants)

After that, Mother Earth Gaea gave birth to the Giants and she advised them to start a new war against Zeus and the Olympians. This time a great hero of Greek mythology helped the Gods. Hercules, the son of Zeus. At last the Giants were defeated and crushed, some being buried under islands.

Zeus against the Giants

TYPHON

Now Mother Earth mated with Tartarus and gave birth to Typhon or Typhoeus, a terrible monster.

He was taller than the mountains and from his shoulders sprang a hundred snake heads, from whose mouths fire came out. He was the last son of Mother Earth. All the Olympians were so afraid that they left Mount Olympus and went to Egypt. Zeus alone was left to face the monster Typhon. The terrible battle lasted for days. Suddenly the monster succeeded in cutting out Zeus' sinews in his hands and feet leaving him helpless. Typhon gave the sinews to a female dragon, called Delphyna, to hide them in a cave. This time one of Zeus' children was to help him - Hermes (Mercury). He stole the sinews back and so Zeus recovered his strength and killed Typhon by striking him with lightning...

Zeus against Typhon.

All ancient authors agreed that Zeus had many female partners and many erotic adventures. A great number of children were born of these unions.

The official wife of Zeus was Hera (Juno). Children of the divine couple were Hebe, Ares (Mars) and Eileithyia. This divine perfect couple were the guardians of marriage, but this does not mean that Zeus was a faithful husband. As we learn from the Homeric Hymn, Zeus did not feel that he needed to be discreet and very often he would flaunt the fact, so Hera became jealous.

According to the Theogony of Hesiod, Zeus' first consort was Metis, goddess of wisdom. When she became pregnant, Zeus devoured her, because he was afraid of the prophecy – as his father Cronus was – that the child of Metis would overpower him.

When time came for Metis to give birth to her child inside Zeus, he felt a terrible headache. Then he asked Hephaistos (Vulcun) to open his head. From the wise head of Zeus then sprang his daughter, goddess Athena (Miverva).

The second wife of Zeus, according to Hesiod, was named Themis, goddess of justice, and so Horai* (Hours) and Moires (Fates) were born.

His third wife the Oceanide Eurynome gave birth to the three Charites (three Graces)*.

Then came the turn of goddess Demeter (Ceres) and so Persephone (Kore) was born.

He mated with the Titaness Mnemosyne (Memory) and the offspring of this wedlock were the nine Muses*.

Next came Leto, daughter of Titans, who gave birth to the twins, Apollo and Artemis (Diana) and the nymph Mea, who gave birth to Hermes.

These were the erotic adventures of

Zeus with goddesses, but he also had erotic relationships with beautiful human beings, most of them daughters of kings. According to the Homeric Hymn, the most famous were: Alcmene who gave birth to Hercules, Semele who gave birth to Dionysus (Bacchus), Leda who gave birth to the twins Dioskouri (sons of Zeus) and beautiful Helen. Danae, who gave birth to Perseus. Europa, who gave birth to Minos, Sarpidon and Rodamanthys.

The Muses, from a vase painting

Zeus was worshipped all over Greece. The most ancient centers of worship were: Dodona in the north of Greece, where the famous oracle was; Arcadia in Peloponessos; the island of Crete; Olympia, the sacred land of the Olympic games.

Great sculptors created magnificent statues of Zeus. He was represented as a powerful and handsome man with thick flowing hair and beard, holding in his hand the sceptre and the eagle.

Other symbols of Zeus were the Aegis (the hide of the goat Amaltheia) and the thunderbolts.

The most glorious statue of Zeus was the one by Phidias at Olympia. It was a seated statue and colossal, (13 m. high) made of gold and ivory, one of the seven wonders of the world.

---

* Horai (Hours): The word means seasons of the year. They are named Eunomia (Law and Order), Dike (Justice) and Eirene (Peace).

* Three Charites (Graces): They were represented as a triad, personifying beauty. They are named Aglaia (Splendor), Euphrosyne (Mirth) and Thalia (Good Cheer).

* Nine Muses: Clio was Muse of history, Urania of astronomy, Melpomene of tragedy, Thalia of comedy, Terpsichore of the dance, Calliope of epic poetry, Erato of love poetry, Polhymnia of songs to the gods and Euterpe of lyric poetry.

HERA
(JUNO)

**"Golden-throned Hera, among immortals the queen.
Chief among them in beauty, the glorious lady.
All the blessed in high Olympus revere, Honor even as Zeus, the lord of the thunder"**

Hera was the queen of Mount Olympus. Sister and lawful wife of Zeus, daughter of Rhea and Cronus.

When she was born, she had the same fate as her brothers and sisters; of being eaten by her father. We have seen how Zeus forced Cronus to bring his children out to the light again.

Hera and Zeus represent in Greek mythology the perfect form of a married couple. Hera was protectress of marriage. Generally, she was the goddess who protected woman – either maiden or as wife.

She was the most grand of all the goddesses and as wife of Zeus, she was respected by all the Olympians.

Hera was brought up on the island of Euboia. From there, Zeus ran away with her and took refuge on Mount Kithairon. According to Homer, every year she used to take a bath in the spring Canathos (at Nauplia), and she became a virgin again. The enthroned first lady of Olympus was exceptionally beautiful, but of a severe type of beauty. The story of Paris is well known. He was the handsome prince of Troy, who had to offer the golden apple to "the most beautiful". Three goddesses, Hera, Athena and Aphrodite, the most beautiful of Olympus claimed the title.

Hera, from a vase painting

21

Hebe, she personified joyful youth

Paris offered the apple to Aphrodite (Venus), the goddess of love,who promised him the most beautiful woman for himself. This was beautiful Helen, the wife of Menelaus, King of Sparta. The abduction of Helen by Paris started the Trojan war. We know that the Olympians played a very important role in this war, some supporting the Greeks, and others the Trojans. Hera, who disliked Paris, went on to fight on the side of the Greeks.

Hera had a strong character and a prominent personality. When Zeus was angry, none of the Olympians had the strength to oppose him. Hera was the only one who dared to. She knew him so well that she could be very diplomatic. She knew how to calm him. Very often the goddess was jealous and Zeus gave her many chances for that.

We have seen his numerous paramours and their offspring – both mortal and immortal. So, Hera became cruel with her rivals. She persecuted them and their children without mercy. For example she pursued Hercules until his death. Once Hera became so angry with Zeus for his behaviour, that she abandoned him and Mount Olympus, and went to the island of Euboea. He begged her to come back without result.

Then Zeus had a very clever plan. He fixed a wooden statue (xoanon) and dressed it with beautiful clothes. Then he informed everybody that this was his new bride.

Hera was so angry that she ripped off the dresses of the statue. She had a surprise when she realised that it was only a trick. Her humour came back and the couple became happy again.

Hera and Zeus gave birth to three children: Hebe, Ares and Eileithyia.

Hebe was the personification of eternal youth. She was the one who offered the "nectar and the ambrosia" to the gods, which stabilized their youth.

When Hercules (after his human death) reached Mount Olympus, he became immortal and received Hebe as wife. Thus, Hercules was reconciled with Hera, who had persecuted him so mercilessly when he was alive.

Hebe gave Hercules two sons, Alexiares and Aniceto.

The second child of Zeus and Hera was Ares (Mars), the god of war (there is a special chapter on him).

Their third child Eileithyia was the goddess of child-birth. A few ancient authors refer to Hephaestos (Vulcan), the god of fire and metal works, as the son of Hera.

The goddess was worshipped all over Greece.

Very famous sanctuaries were on the island of Samos, in Athens, Eleusis, Corinth, Epidaurus, Nemea, Argos, Olympia, Sparta and in the Greek cities of Sicily Acragas and Selenus. The one on the island of Samos had one of the largest temples in her honour.

In the sanctuary of Argos was her most famous statue, work of the great sculptor Polycleitos.

According to the traveller Pausanias, the goddess in this statue was seated on a gold and ivory throne. One hand held the scepter and the other hand held the pomegranate.

The sceptre symbolized her strength as queen of all gods and mortals, and the pomegranate symbolized fertility.

Other symbols of the goddess were the cuckoo and the peacock, which symbolized in accordance with the schools of thought the star-studded skies, or the mythical Argus.

Great festivals were celebrated in many Greek cities in her honour, the so called "Heraea", but in addition there were the "Daedala", the "Kallisteia" and the "He - catombaea".During these festivals, besides the cult and the sacrifices, they held athletic games and beauty contests.

Hera and Zeus represent in Greek mythology, the perfect form of a married couple

POSEIDON
(NEPTUNE)

Poseidon was a powerful god who ruled over the sea. In addition he was the patron of fresh water (sources, rivers and springs), the god of earthquakes and the giver of horses to man.

From ancient times the Greeks were a seafaring people. So it was quite logical to worship marine gods – Poseidon being the most important. He was son of Cronus and Rhea, brother of Zeus and Hades. We know already that Poseidon was devoured by his father and Zeus forced Cronus to bring him, along with his brothers, out of his stomach.

Zeus, the god of justice, drew lots portioning off the rule of the universe to himself and his brothers. Poseidon became lord of the sea, Hades became the King of the underworld, while he himself became ruler of the sky. Mount Olympus and the Earth were commonly shared.

The palace of Poseidon, "of gleaming gold", was deep in the Aegean sea. Poseidon's wife was one of the Nereids*, the beautiful Amphitrite.

According to the ancient authors, one day Amphitrite was playing with her sisters, the other Nereids on the island of Naxos. When Poseidon saw her, he fell in love and married her. She thus became the queen of the sea. The couple gave birth to the Triton* and to many nymphs.

* Nereids: Sea-maidens, daughters of Nereus and Doris, the Oceanide. Nereus their father, was the wise and kind "Old Man" of the sea, who predicted Poseidon.
* Triton: He was the trumpeter of the Sea. His trumpet was a great shell. Triton was half man, half fish, with two tails; he had prophetic powers.

Poseidon holding the trident and a dolphin

Marble statue of Poseidon, National Museum of Athens

Like his brother Zeus, so Poseidon had many love affairs. He was luckier though, as Amphitrite was not as jealous as Hera.

There was only one occasion when Poseidon fell in love with the nymph Skylla. To take revenge, Amphitrite, threw a magic herb in the water of the spring where the nymph took her bath, transforming her to an awful monster.

Generally, we can say that Poseidon's children were cruel and savage people or monsters. Here is a list of them.

Antaeos was the cruel King of Libya. He built a temple in Poseidon's honour, with the bones of the unlucky people that he had killed. This savage giant was killed by Hercules.

Vousiris, became famous for his cruelty in Egypt, where he killed every stranger who entered his country. He was killed by Hercules as well.

Amycos, used to do the same thing at Bethenia. He was an outstanding pugilist (he was the one who invented pugilism). All strangers visiting his country were obliged to contend with him and they were killed. He was killed by Polux*.

The thief Cercyon, was the king of Eleusis. Many people were killed by him until Theseus stopped him. The same great hero, Theseus, killed three other sons of Poseidon, all famous for their cruelties. They were Skiron, Sinis and Procroustis. They caused a lot of trouble to the travellers that had to follow the road from Athens to Corinth.

We must mention also the winged horse "Pegasus", who was son of Medusa and Poseidon.

Ending the list we refer to the Cyclop Polyphemos. It is well known that Odysseus (Ulysses) on the way back from the Trojan war, blinded the Giant. His father Poseidon became so angry, that poor Odysseus for ten years desperately contended with the sea until he arrived at his beloved fatherland, the island of Ithaca.

When Poseidon was angry, the sea became rough, as the god was erupting the water with his trident and set the winds free. So he created the tempests and the sea monsters came out from the enormous waves and brought great fear to people.

When the god became happy, the sea was quiet and peaceful, dolphins play-

Poseidon and Amphitrite

ed in the blue waters and the beautiful Nereids danced joyfully...

The Greeks, before starting a trip, prayed to Poseidon, to "be kindly in heart and help those who voyage in ships". The sailors and the fishermen used to do the same.

After a sea battle, they had to offer him thanksgivings, as it was thought that the victory was given by the god. In the year 373 B.C., a terrible earthquake and a tidal wave destroyed the two cities, Eliki and Boupe. People then thought that it was Poseidon's anger for the disobedience of the inhabitants to the god.

---

* Polux: (Polydeuces) and his brother Castor were a very popular pair in Greek mythology, they were sons of Leda and Zeus, and were often called the "Dioscouri".

As the god of the sea, Poseidon was worshipped especially near the sea coasts and capes. Well known are his quarrels with Athena for the possession of Athens, with Helios for Corinth and Hera for Argos.

Very famous sanctuaries to Poseidon in Asia Minor were the one of Mycaly and the one of Poseidonia (Troezenia).

Another center of his worship was on the island of Thera (Santorini), where they often had earthquakes and volcanic eruptions. Near the canal of Corinth at the Isthmia was the most famous centre of his worship. There were held panhellenic festivals, "the Isthmia" in his honour.

Other temples of the god existed at Patras, Eliki, Aege, Aegion and the is-land of Aegina. The sanctuary most well known to us, is the one at Cape Sounion at the southern part of the mainland of Attica. One stands breathless looking at the Acropolis of Sounion, crowned by the magnificent marble temple of Poseidon of the 5th century B.C.

In art, Poseidon is depicted as a dignified and handsome god with thick flowing hair and beard. Most of his statues resemble Zeus and so very often we have difficulties indentifying them as either Zeus or Poseidon.

Sacred symbols of Poseidon are the trident, the tuna fish and the dolphin. Two great sculptors of the 4th B.C. Scopas and Lysippos made statues of the god.

Tritons. The one holding an oar, the other an anchor

HADES
(PLUTON)*

He was the third son of Cronus. When he was born he was devoured by his father, until Zeus set him free. When Zeus overthrew Cronus the three brothers had to share the universe.

It is mentioned already that Zeus became the master of heavens, Poseidon, the god of the eternal sea and Hades the king of the underworld. So, Hades was the lord of the land of the dead and the supreme judge. He was, a terrible, but not an evil God.

According to Homer "...his kingdom was so deep in the earth as far as earth is from the sky...".

Nearby were the gates of the setting sun. The entrance to the land of dead was at the meeting place of the rivers Acheron (the Woeful), Pyriphlegethon (the Fiery), Kokytos (the Wailing) and Lethe (Forgetfulness).

The boundary was usually the river Styx (the abhorrent). To cross the Styx or (according to other ancient authors) Acheron, the dead had to pay the ferryman namely Charon. This is the reason that the dead were buried with a coin in their mouth. As soon as they crossed the river, the dead were led to judgement and then they were assigned to the appropriate place.

Finally, the entrance of the House of Hades was guarded by Kerberos, the watch-dog of the underworld "...with a voice of bronze and three heads..."

At the very early times Hades was a dark figure and people were afraid even to mention his name. Through the

Kerberos, the three headed dog
of the underworld

* Hades (Pluton): Both are Greek names. Pluton means wealth. The Romans as well as the Greeks called him by this name, but often they translated it into Dis, the Latin word for rich.

29

**Pluton, he also offered people, prosperity
and riches**

Keres*, the Harpies*, and the Erinyes*,
who were his servants and messengers.
According to Homeric Hymn, once
coming out, Hades met beautiful
Persephone (Proserpina) or Kore, who
was the only daughter of Demeter, the
goddess of agriculture.

Persephone herself was the younger
replica of her mother, a goddess of the
fertility of the earth.

The beautiful maiden was playing with
her girlfriends in a green and flowering
meadow. Hades fell in love with her
immediately. Mother-Earth then, to
satisfy him, gave birth to an extraordi-
narily beautiful narcissus flower.

Persephone, saw the magnificent flower
and at the moment she went to pick it,
the earth opened and Hades came out in
his chariot, pulled by the immortal
horses. He seized Persephone, he took
her to his dark Kingdom, and made her
queen of the Underworld. Thus,
Persephone had a double character; as
goddess of the dead and as a goddess of
the fertility of the earth.

Hades was not very often represented
in art. The few statues of the god resemble his brother Zeus, same in expression. Seneka* says that "he hath Jove's

centuries though, cruel Hades who put
fear in human beings, became a god
that people started to understand. He
was king of the Dead – not Death himself, whom the Greeks called Thanatos.
Especially, during the classical period
and under the influence of the Eleusinian Mysteries, Hades was not only the
god of the dead, but on him depended
the fertility of the earth, and he was
appealed by the cultivators of the soil
to aid them in the fertility and the rich-
ness of the crop. Also, all things that the
earth offered, were his own gifts, inclu-
ding metals and minerals. Thus, he
offered people prosperity and riches.

The god appeared always with his helmet Kini*, which made him invisible. He
rarely came out of his kingdom. He pre-
fered to live there, far from Olympus
and the Olympians, surrounded by the
divinities of the underworld, such as the

---

* Kini: Type of helmet made of dog skin

---

* Keres: Dark spirits of death and revenge, called
"daughters of Hades".

* Harpies: Underworld deities, whose number
varies. Initially, there were two, Aelo and Ocy-
pete. Later on was added Celaeno. They were
extraordinary beautiful with wings that helped
them to fly as envoys of Hades.
Through the centuries though, they changed
shape and character. They became such dreadful creatures that they seized their human victims
and carried them off to Hades.

* Erinyes: Underworld winged deities, dressed
with long dark robes. Guardians of oaths, they
punished all perjurers. There were three in number: Alecto (she who cannot be opposed),
Tisiphone (the avenger of murder) and Megaira
(the spirit of hatred).

* Seneka: Roman poet and philosopher of the 1st
century A.D.

own look, but Jove's when he doth thunder".

A sacred plant dedicated to Hades was the mint, the Greek mynthe. According to the legend, Mynthe was a beautiful Nymph of the underworld, and Hades fell in love with her. Persephone then persecuted her and so Hades transformed her to a plant, the mint.

Similar is the legend about the poplar, the Greek leuce. Leuce was daughter of the Ocean, and Hades fell in love with her. When the girl died, he transformed her to a poplar-tree.

Other sacred plants dedicated to the god were the cypress-tree and the narcissus. From the animals we can mention the dog, the wolf and the snake.

There were only a few places that the god was worshipped. We know about the one in Elis on Peloponnesos. But even this sanctuary was open only once a year, and had only one priest.

There were many caves and precipices though dedicated to Hades, under the name Plutonia or Charonia. Most of these sanctuaries were Oracles as well. We can divide them into necromantia (necromancies) and medical oracles.

An Eriny holding a snake and a miror

Very often the god was worshipped in combination with his wife Persephone and her mother Demeter, as for example at Eleusis.

Persephone and Hades

Demeter, Triptolemos and Persephone, National Museum of Athens

DEMETER
(CERES)

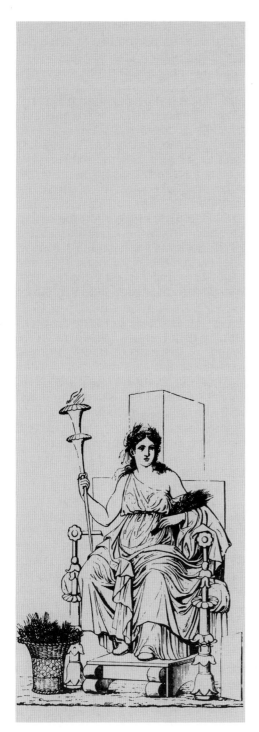

Demeter, mural painting from Pompeii

Demeter or Demetra was the goddess of agriculture and cultivation of the earth. We can characterise her as a special form of the preexisted Mother Earth. She assisted with the harvesting and ensured that crops matured. Finally, she was the one who taught people the way to sow wheat, corn and barley. Demeter was the daughter of Cronus and Rhea. She was swallowed by her father Cronus, as her brothers and sisters, until Zeus forced him to set them free from his stomach.

Her two brothers, Zeus and Poseidon, fell in love with her, but the modest goddess refused their love.

Once, Zeus was transformed into a bull and ravished her, so her beautiful daughter Persephone or Kore was born. To avoid her second brother Poseidon, Demeter was transformed into a mare, but then, the god ravished her, by transforming himself into a horse, and so she bore the steed Arion.

According to the Roman poet Obedius, there is only one time that the goddess fell in love. He was a hero called Jassion, and so the goddess gave birth to Plutus (riches, wealth; not to be confused with Hades-Pluton).

Plutus, wandered around the world, offering abundance and riches to mortals.

We have already talked about Hades and the beloved daughter of Demeter, Persephone. This is one of the most famous legends of Greek mythology (see chapter on Hades).

As soon as Persephone disappeared, her bereaved mother, lit two torches and wandered all over the world searching for her. According to the Homeric Hymn "... she was so unhappy that she

33

tore off her ribbons and put on her shoulders a black shawl ...".

She was marching all over, days and nights, but no human or god dared to tell her the truth.

"... For nine days and nights she wandered and she refused to eat or drink "nectar and ambrosia" and she did not take a bath ...".

The tenth day she met Helius (the Sun), who had seen everything and told her who had carried off her daughter. The mother goddess, full of indignation against Zeus and the gods in general, abandoned Mount Olympus and continued her wanderings on the earth, un-

**Demeter and Triptolemos,
from a vase painting**

til she arrived at Eleusis*.

She took the form of an old lady that nobody could recognize. She sat down to rest near the well Parthenion, not far from the Palace of King Keleos, the King of Eleusis.

The daughters of the King invited her to the palace, and the mother queen Metaneira, employed her to nurse her son Demophon*. The goddess, every night, secretly rubbed the baby with ambrosia and laid him in the fire to make him immortal and invulnerable. Unfortunately, Metaneira discovered one night what the goddess was doing to her son and screamed with terror. The goddess then took her own form, explained to Metaneira she meant no harm to the baby and asked that rites should be instituted in her honour. Thus, she taught them her secret rites, the famous Eleusinian Mysteries. Then the goddess left Eleusis with her heart full of sorrow. The earth refused to give fruits and vegetation. Animals started to die. That year was the most dreadful and cruel for mankind all over the earth. Then, Zeus decided to interfere and solve the problem. He sent Hermes, the winged messenger of the gods to Hades. Hermes persuaded him to allow Persephone to come out from his dark Kingdom for half of each year and be reunited with her beloved mother.

Before Persephone left, her busband gave her the seed of pomegranate to eat. That was to bring her back again to him, for the other half of the year. Thus, she became a goddess of the dead and also a goddess of fertility of the earth.

Many festivals were celebrated in Demeter's honour: The "Thesmophoria" according to Herodotus*, lasted three days. Only married women could participate, and in their duration it was not allowed for them to have any sexual relations. Other famous festivals in her honour the "Aloa", the "Chloeia", the "Sacred Arosis" and the most famous of

---

* Eleusis: A site about 20 km from Athens, where archeologists have excavated Demeter's sanctuary.

* Demophon: or according to Ovid his name was Triptolemos. He became her messenger to carry the seed of wheat through the world.
* Herodotus: "The father of History" as he is usually called. He was the first to write "history". He was born in Alicarnassus in the year 484 B.C.

them all, the "Eleusinian Mysteries", that were held every year at Eleusis.

"Queen of fragrant Eleusis,
Giver of earth's good gifts,
Give me your grace, O Demeter,
You, too, Persephone, Fairest,
Maiden all lovely, I offer
song for your favour".

The inititated were not allowed to talk about rites. From recent research and evidence, we conclude, that in the "Telestirion" (a kind of theatre) they reenacted the main episodes of the goddess' life.

The initiated assured her protection throughout life and the privilige of a happy life after death.

"Thice-blessed are those mortals who Having seen the rituals leave for Hades, for
They can be sure of a good life there. As for
The Others, only evil awaits them"
(Sophocles)

The sacred symbols of the goddess were the wheat, the poppy and the snake.
The great sculptors of the classical period, like Phidias and Praxiteles, created magnificent statues of the goddess and her daughter Persephone.
A famous relief, work of Phidias, is in the National Archeological Museum of Athens. Other statues are preserved in the Louvre, Capitolium, Naples and Copenhagen.

Persephone and Hermes coming out from the dark Kingdom of Hades

Bronze statue of Athena, Museum of Pireus

ATHENA
(MINERVA)

Pallas* Athena was the goddess of wisdom, the patron goddess of the arts and all types of work. She was a virgin goddess (Parthenos), with a stern but kind beauty. Her birth was unusually strange, as she was not born from a female goddess, but from Zeus himself.

According to Hesiod, Zeus accepted as consort Metis, who was the most wise of all gods and humans. This was a dangerous union though, for Metis was destined to bear, first Athena and then a god who should rule Olympus.

Thus, Zeus swallowed her before the birth of Athena, who in due time was born from his head.

According to the Homeric Hymn, when the time came for Athena to be born, Zeus suffered from a terrible headache. He ordered Hephaestos (Vulcan), the god of fire and metal works, to open his head with his axe. From there out came in full armour shouting her war cry, his most wise daughter, Athena. Mount Olympus and the seas began shaking and Zeus was pleased ... Athena became his beloved child.

One of the most famous Greek legends, is the episode between Athena and Poseidon about the possesion of Attica. The quarrel ended with the contest be-

* Pallas: This title was given to Athena from the giant Pallas, whom she killed in the battle against the giants.
According to another version though, Pallas was the favourite companion of Athena. She was the daughter of Tritonis, who brought up the goddess. During a quarrel Pallas was killed by Athena, who in despair created a wooden statue of her and put on it the aigis, which was Athena's shield, made of goat's skin.
Since then, they called "Palladia" all the sacred statues of Athena, which were believed to have dropped from heaven.

From the head of Zeus out came
in full armour, Athena

Athena, from a vase painting

tween the two gods. The one who would offer the greatest and most useful present to the city, would become the owner of the land.

Thus, Poseidon stood on top of the Acropolis of Athens, struck the rock with his trident and produced a horse, the first ever seen.

According to another account, he produced a salt spring. When Athena's turn came, she struck the ground with her spear and the earth offered an olive tree, the symbol of peace. The judges, gods and humans, pronounced Athena's gift acceptable. In gratitude, the inhabitants named their city Athens*. The beloved goddess Athena was always ready to protect her city. Under her protection the greatest values of civilization flourished in Athens: the supreme intellect and the gentle arts of living.

The Athenians to show their love and affection, built on top of the sacred rock of the Acropolis in Athens the master-piece of the centuries – the Parthenon, the temple of the goddess.

According to Homer, Athena took part in the Trojan war, protecting the Greeks and her favorite heroes. She stood by Diomides and she made flames come from his helmet and shield. When Achilles was in danger, she protected him in a fiery cloud. She helped Odysseus (Ulysses) on the way back from the Trojan war to reach his beloved Ithaca.

Generally, she was the patroness of the famous heroes in their difficult moments. She stood by Hercules and helped him with her useful advice. Another famous hero, Perseus killed the monster Gorgon* with her help. Perseus, to thank the goddess, offered her the head of the monster (gorgonion).

She helped also another hero, Bellerophon, to catch and tame the magnificent winged horse Pegasos, giving him a celestial bridle. Finally, she taught Argos to build the famous ship "Argo", which carried Jason and the Argonauts

---

* Athens: Athens had previously been called Kekropia from Kekrops, a legendery King of Athens.

* Gorgon: The Gorgon Meduss was a dreadful monster. She had snakes instead of hair. Her teeth were of a wild boar's, and her eyes so awful that anyone who dared to look at her was turned to stone.

Athena

The Acropolis of Athens. The Athenians built on top

of the sacred rock, the masterpieces of the centuries

41

to Colhis, in order to bring back to Greece the "golden fleece".

This magnificent virgin goddess Athena, was the beloved deity of the Greek people. She was worshipped all over the mainland, Asia Minor and South Italy.

We must mention a few of her titles:

Athena Promachos (Champion), Athena Polias (goddess of the City), Athena Boulaia (she of the Counsil), Athena

The Gorgon turned all who looked on her to stone

Ergane (Worker). Under her last title she was the goddess of handicrafts.

She was the one who taught people the arts of spinning, weaving, embroidery, carving, gold work, architecture. She protected also the potters and the shoemakers.

Great festivals were held in her honor. The most famous was "the Great Panathenaea" in Athens. They lasted for ten days. During the festival, they held athletic games, musical contests, horse races, dance contests and a contest of male beauty.

The most magnificent part of this festival was the "Panathenaean procession". The procession started from one of the gates of Athens, the Dipylon gate, crossed the Agora (the ancient market place) and following the Sacred Way, arrived on top of the Acropolis in order to offer the new hand-woven golden "peplos" (veil), to Athena.

People that visit the Acropolis in our days, can see on the frieze of the Parthenon (a great part of the original is preserved in the museum of the Acropolis) the procession, which was the work of Pheidias, the greatest sculptor of the classical period. One can see the magistrates and the generals in parade, the animals for the sacrifices slowly following their guides, the beautiful virgins of Athens carrying gracefully the vessels and baskets full of gifts and offerings to the beloved goddess, and the handsome youths of the fifth century B.C. conducting the horses and the chariots. This admirable procession was done in honor of the most perfect deity that human imagination could create.

Sacred symbols of the goddess were the spear, the owl, the snake and the olive tree.

She was represented in art as a stately maiden with a beautiful but severe face, blue-grey eyes and a powerful but graceful body. Usually, she was shown fully armoured with a helmet, a long spear and a shield on which was the Gorgon's face.

Great sculptors created marvelous statues of the goddess. One can distinguish two different types of the goddess. The first represents her seated, and the second standing. When she is sitting she is the goddess of peace, while standing she is a war goddess*.

The most famous statues of Athena were works of Pheidias. The most perfect stood in the middle of the Parthenon, 12 m. high, of gold and ivory.

---

* War goddess, but only to defend the state and the home from outside enemies. Thus, she does not have the rough character of Ares (Mars) the god of War.

Athena and Poseidon

Marble statue of Apollo, Museum of Olympia

APOLLO

The Belvedere Apollo, Vatican Museum

Apollo was the most characteristically Greek of all the Olympian gods; the perfect example of male Greek beauty. Charming, strong, brave and clever. He was the god of the sun and light, the patron of truth, archery, music (particularly that of the lyre). He was also the healer, who taught men the healing art. Apollo was the son of Zeus and Leto (Latona), the daughter of Titans. According to Hesiod, Zeus fell in love with Leto and of course his wife Hera became very jealous.

In order to take revenge, when time came for Leto to give birth to the twins, Apollo and Artemis (see chapter on Artemis), Hera did not permit Earth to give her a place. Desperate Leto, wandered all over the world, but all lands and islands refused to accept her, afraid of Hera's wrathful commands.

At last, Poseidon, the god of the sea, had pity on her and he revealed the island of Delos, which until then was under the sea. Even so, Hera did not permit her daughter, Eileithyia, the goddess of child-birth, to assist poor Leto.

The Homeric Hymn says that nine days and nine nights she suffered, finally Eileithyia arrived at the island of Delos and there, under a tree, Leto gave birth to her twins, Apollo and Artemis.

As soon as Apollo was four days old, he left Mt. Olympus and he reached Mt. Parnassus. There he killed the dragon "Python" and he became the master of the place called Delphi: which before his coming belonged to mother Earth. There, Apollo founded his famous oracle. The Homeric Hymn to Apollo says "... to you was given by Zeus the knowing of the fate and prophecy ...".

The site of Delphi, with an altitude of

Delphi

The Sanctuary of Apollo

about 600 metres above sea level, became the most famous sanctuary of Apollo; it was the "omphalos" of the earth (the middle point of the earth). As soon as the god became the absolute master of this holy land, he needed priests for his sanctuary.

According to the Homeric Hymn always, he looked down the blue sea of Itea (the ancient bay of Krissa), and saw a boat from the island of Crete, near the coast.

Apollo then was transformed into a dolphin and in a divine way forced the boat to dock at Krissa. He asked the sailors to stay there for ever and they became his first priests.

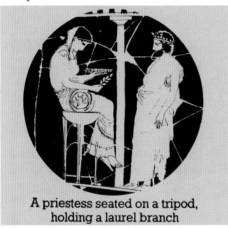

A priestess seated on a tripod, holding a laurel branch

People that visit Delphi in our days and walk in the sanctuary of Apollo, can feel the everlasting glory of this sacred place, the breath-taking scenery with the wild rocks of Phaedryades and the peaceful water of the spring Castalia, the silvergreen plain of the valley of Pleistos, where centuries now the old olive-trees bear their fruits; and further away at the end of the mountain chain, the sparkling blue water of the Corinthian bay.

Let us describe now the proceedings at the sancruary of Apollo 2,500 years ago, when the crowds of the ancient world arrived here for advice. It did not make any difference if the oracle was addres-

sing a whole city-state or just one person. The ceremony was always the same.

First Pythia, the priestess, took a bath in the waters of the spring Castalia to purify her body. Then, she drank the water of the spring Cassotis to purify her soul. The priestess, dressed with the long robe of Apollo, approached the altar, where the priests sacrificed the animals. Then she entered the temple, she chewed laurel leaves and sat on the golden tripod (a three legged stool), which stood on top of a chasm from where gusts of strange vapors came out. She fell in ecstasy and inspired by Apollo she gave the prophecy...

"O Phoebus, from your throne of truth, from your dwelling-place at the heai t of the world, you speak to men. By Zeus's decree no lie comes there, no shadow to darken the world of truth".

To thank the god for the oracles, people offered him thanks. A magnificent collection of statues, reliefs and inscriptions decorated both sides of the "Sacred Way", the path to the Temple. The rich Greek cities built along this passage the famous treasuries, and so Delphi became the "Bank of Greece". With the "Amphictionic League" that was organized at Delphi, we have for first time, the idea of the United Nations. Great festivals were held at Delphi in Apollo's honor. The best known were the "Pythian Games"*, which were celebrated with great magnificence, to commemmorate the victory of the god over the dragon Python.

This is the reason that they named him Pythian Apollo. A few other epithets often given him were "Pheobus", (brilliant); "Delian" as his birthplace was the island of Delos; "Cynthian", from Mt.

---

* Similar to the Olympic Games at Olympia, and the Nemean Games at Nemea.

Cynthus in Delos; and "Hyperborius". This last title was given to Apollo because every year during the three months of winter the god deserted Delphi, flying on a swan-chariot to the country of the Hyperboreans, which means the land beyond the cold North Wind. According to the Pythian Ode of Pindar

"Neither by ship nor on foot couldst thou find the wondrous way to the assembly of the Hyperboreans".

In this blessed country people lived for a thousand years. They knew no disease and war and they passed their time playing the lyre and the flute.
Besides his power of divination, Apollo

Apollo playing his golden lyre

was the master musician who delighted the Olympians as he played on his golden lyre. The songs and hymns in his honor were always accompanied by this musical instrument. As god of music, Apollo is always followed by the Muses and Charites.
Apollo was a great lover! He had many erotic adventures, but most of them had not a happy end. Well known is his desperate passion for the Nymph Daphne (Laurel), daughter of the Ladon River (or Peneos) and Earth. The beautiful Nymph preferred to be turned to a laurel-tree than to accept his love. Since then, the laurel became his sacred plant.
Some other love adventures of Apollo were with: The Nymph Melia, daughter

of Oceanus, who gave him a son, Isminon; The Nymph Korykian, who gave birth to the god Sycorea, who founded Sycoreia on Mt. Parnassus; Goddess Hestia*, who refused his love taking the oath of perpetual virginity.
Cassandra, daughter of King Priam; Marpessa, who preferred the mortal Ida to Apollo; Voline, who preferred to be drowned in the sea rather than to accept his love; Castalia, a beautiful girl from Delphi, who threw herself into the spring, which since then was named Castalia; Coronis, the daughter of Phlegyas, who gave birth to the great godhero Asklepios (Aesculapius there is a special chapter on him); Kreusa, daughter of Erechtheus, who gave birth to Ion, the head of the race of the Ionians; Kerene, daughter of Ipseos, King of the Lapithes, who bore the god Aristeon, worshipped in Arcadia; Akakalis, the daughter of Minos, King of Crete, who gave birth to many sons. Two of them, became famous. The one founded the city of Naxos while the other founded Miletos.
Apollo was worshipped all over Greece. Other famous oracles, besides the one of Delphi, were at Acraephis, in Thebes, in Argos, and the one of Miletos in Asia Minor.
His sacred plants were the laurel, the palm-tree and the myrtle. From the birds he preferred the swan, the hawk and the vulture. He also loved the dolphin, the wolf, the mouse, the snake and the lizard. Other symbols of the god were the tripod, the bow and arrow.
Great sculptors like Canahos, Calamis, Myron, Scopas and Praxiteles, created magnificent statues of Apollo.

---

* Hestia (Vesta): The goddess of Hearth, daughter of Cronus and Rhea. She was the goddess of the family hearth, the symbol of the home, but also of the public hearth of every city-state. In all the prayers her name was first recited. "Hestia, in all dwellings of men and immortals, yours is the highest honor, the sweet wine offered. First and last at the feast poured out to you duly...".

Artemis, marble relief from Vravron

ARTEMIS
(DIANA)

Artemis was the twin sister of Apollo, daughter of Leto and Zeus. It is already mentioned (see chapter Apollo), that Leto suffered by Hera's jealousy and how she finally succeeded in giving birth to her twins, on the island of Delos. It is said that Artemis was born first and that she helped her mother to give birth to Apollo.

There are many theories about her origin. We know that she was worshipped in Western Asia Minor and in Minoan Crete. In Asia Minor she was a goddess of fertility, while in Crete she was Mother Earth. Homer calls her "Potnia Thiron", meaning Mistress of Wild Animals. The Hellenic spirit though, altered her character and according to the Homeric Hymn, she was the goddess of hunting and nature, and also the "protectress of youth".

She was called "Cynthia" from her birth place Mt. Cynthus in Delos. Very often she was called "Locheia", as she helped women in childbirth by easing their pain.

Artemis was one of the three maiden goddesses of Olympus, accorting to the Hymn

"Golden Aphrodite who stirs with
love all creation, cannot bend
nor esnare three hearts:
the pure maiden Hestia,
Grey-eyed Athena who cares but
for war and the arts of the
craftsmen,
Artemis, lover of woods and the
wild chase over the mountain".

There is a very famous story that took place at the beginning of the Trojan war. The Greek fleet was ready in Aulis of Attica to start the long voyage to Troy, in

Artemis, godess of the hunt
and patroness of beasts

order to bring back beautiful Helen, the wife of Menelaus, King of Sparta, who was taken to Troy by Paris. For days, the Greek fleet was left stranded as there was no breeze to blow their sails.

King Agamemnon of Mycenae, the leader of the expedition, asked Calhas, the seer, the reason why there was no breeze. Calhas answered that goddess Artemis was angry and she would permit their departure only if Agamemnon sacrificed his daughter Iphigenia (Iphigenia in Aulis). Finally, Agamemnon was obliged to bring from Mycenae his daughter. The moment the priest was ready to sacrifice the innocent virgin, Artemis appeared, seized Iphigenia from the altar and left in her place a deer.

Then the goddess transported her to Taurus (Iphigenia in Tauris) where one of her sanctuaries was and there she became a priestess of the goddess. Tauris (in Cremea) was not a very civilised country, as there were held human sacrifices. It was a misfortune for a stranger to reach this land.

Years later, Iphigenia's brother Orestes, searching for her, arrived in Tauris, accompanied by his friend Pyladis. Both of them were held to be sacrificed by the priestess of Artemis. Finally, Iphigenia, with the help of Athena, recognised her brother, and to save him, they left the country by ship, bringing with them the sacred statue of Artemis. The fugitives, arrived at Vravron (east Attica) where Iphigenia founded the famous sanctuary of the goddess and became her first priestess; Thus, the epithet of Artemis "Vravronia".

From the many festivals dedicated to Artemis, the greatest were the "Vravronia". The ceremory was conducted with bears because of the following story.

A tame bear which was dedicated to Artemis wondered round in the city. A young girl treated the animal in a bad way and the bear tore her to pieces. The girl's brother then, killed the animal.

The goddess Artemis got very angry at this sacrilege and spread a plague all over the plain of Attica. The Athenians asked the oracle what they had to do to stop the plague. The answer was that they had to dedicate to Artemis their little daughters in the form of a bear. So, once a year the little girls of Athens from five to ten years of age, dressed like bears, had to stay and serve the goddess, at least once in their life, before getting married. The girls were called "arkti" (little she-bears).

Other famous sanctuaries of the goddess were in Arcadia and many Greek islands, Eubea, Delos; Paros, Samos, Corfu, Crete. On the coast of Asia Minor was the well-known "Artemission of Ephesos".

The goddess was very often worshipped together with her brother Apollo. As she was a goddess of nature, her sanctuaries were in plains, on mountains, near springs and rivers, even near coasts and capes.

It is already mentioned that Artemis was the beloved goddess of young people. In some of her sanctuaries, young girls on their wedding day offered her a lock of their hair or their beloved toys.

Sacred plants of the goddess were the laurel, the cypress, the palm-tree, the myrtle and the cedar.

Her beloved domestic animals were the dog, the goat, the hare and especially the deer. From the wild animals she especially loved the bear, the boar, the lion and the wolf.

It is said that in one of the parks which was dedicated to Artemis, the wild and domestic animals lived together in perfect peace.

Famous sculptors, like Pheidias, Alcamenes, Praxiteles and Menearchos, created incomparable works of art inspired by the virgin goddess. The best known type is the one by Praxiteles, which represents the goddess as a huntress and personifies virginity and modesty.

HERMES
(MERCURY)

He was one of the most beloved deities of Greek mythology. He was the god for everything! His worship started on Mt. Cyllene of Arcadia (Peloponnese) where he was born. Son of Zeus and the Nymph Maia, the daughter of Atlas*, Hermes had many functions. He was the winged messenger of the gods; the god of speech and intelligence. He was also connected with human fertility as it is shown from his old cult-monuments "the Phallus".

He was the god of luck as he gave wealth, honest or dishonest, because he protected traders as well as thieves. The thieves were let free, paying a certain amount of money, called "the money for Hermes".

We must not forget that he was the Master Thief who started upon his career before he was a day old!

"The babe was born at the break of day
and ere the night fell he had stolen away Apollo's herds..."

According to the fourth Homeric Hymn, Hermes was born in a cave. Immediately after his birth, he left his cradle, walked out and met a tortoise. He took its shell and added seven strings from a sheep's intestines and thus the lyre was invented.

This was done in the morning. In the evening he walked out again from his cave and he stole Apollo's cattle and hid them in a cavern. Then he flew quickly back and tucked himself in his cradle. His brother Apollo who had the power of divination knew who the thief was, but

Hermes stole Apollo's cattle

* Atlas: The son of the Titan Japetus and the Oceanide Clymene. Zeus punished him giving him the heavens to support.

Hermes by Praxiteles - Marble statue, Museum of Olympia

the baby Hermes who was a perfect actor denied the accusation and accepted to go to Mt. Olympus to be judged by their father Zeus. Even then, in front of the father of gods and mortals, he continued to lie with such conviction that Zeus started to laugh.

Then he ordered Hermes to search round with Apollo for the lost flock. Finally, the baby thief was obliged to show the cave were the cows were and to appease his brother, he played the lyre and sang with his divine voice.

as he was always ready to serve and help them.

Hermes was close to the mortals and he was a great benefactor, as he invented for them so many useful things. He was the father of astronomy and of mathematics; he invented measures and weights. He gave people the first laws.

Hermes was also the special god of young men. He was the one who founded athletic games. In every gymnasium there was a "Hermai"* (or herm). Besides the gymnasium, the hermai were

Hermes holding Kerykeion (caduceus)

Apollo was so excited that he forgot immediately what had happened. At last, they became beloved friends and the two brothers exchanged magnificent gifts. Hermes offered him the lyre, and Apollo gave Hermes the "golden cane" of the abundance and happiness. There was not only the case of Apollo though. From Poseidon Hermes stole his trident; from Aphrodite her belt and even from Zeus he had the audacity to steal his scepter! Generally however, Hermes was loved by all the Olympians

erected everywhere as boundaries in the Agora, at city gates, on bridges, crossroads and on country roads, to show the way to travellers, as he was their guardian and kept them on the right track.

Under the name "Psyhopompos" (guide of souls). Hermes guided the souls to the underworld. People loved Hermes and they often sacrificed in his honour. They

* Hermai: Square pilars, crowned with a human head, having a phallus at the bottom.

offered him cakes and boiled vegetables.

According to the Homeric Hymn, Hermes fell in love with the beautiful Nymph Dryope, and so the god Pan was born (see chapter Pan).

Another Nymph, Akakalis, gave birth to his son Cydon, the founder on Cydonia on the island of Crete.

According to Apollodoros, Hermes fell in love with Erse, the daughter of Kekrops, king of Athens, and so was born Kephalos, the handsome hunter who was loved by Eos*.

From his love affairs though, the most famous was with Aphrodite herself. The Nymph seized him in her arms so tightly that the two bodies became one. Salmakis prayed that she might always be united to him, and the combination of lover and loved into a single person (hermaphrodite) was born.

Hermes was worshipped all round Greece. His main sanctuaries, except the one of Arcadia, were at Pheneo and Tegea.

His sacred plants were the poppy, the olive-tree and the myrtle. His sacred animals were the ram, the boar and the he-goat.

The most famous festivals in his honor were called "Hermea", where young

Hermes, Hera and Satyrs

two deities were often associated in cult. According to Ovid, they were the parents of a bi-sexual godling, Hermaphroditos. The youth looked very much like his father, but also his mother, so they gave him both names, Hermes and Aphrodite, Hermaphrodite. A young Nymph of a lake, Salmakis, fell in love with the handsome youth, and one day that he was bathing in the lake, the

boys and girls participated in athletic games.

Other symbols of the god were: the "petassus", a broad rimmed hat which had wings on either side. Ancient travellrs and people of the countryside wore the same type of hat.

There were also the "winged golden sandals", which transported him immediately whereever he wanted to be, the "Kerykeion", a type of cane, decorated with snakes with which he could put everyone to sleep when he wanted, and finally the phallus.

In art, Hermes was represented like his brother Apollo, but younger and less

* Eos (the Dawn, Latin Aurora): She was the daughter of Hyperion and Theia. They imagined her driving her chariot. She was called also Rosy-fingered or Saffron-robed (epithets given by Homer).

muscular.

The greatest sculptors of the classical and hellenistic periods created magnificent statues of him. At the museum of Olympia exists a masterpiece by Praxiteles, which represents the god as an "ephebos" (youth), holding in his left arm the baby Dionysos (Bacchus). This wonderful piece of art was found in 1877, during the excavations of Olympia.

Another famous statue of the god, work of the great sculptor Lyssipos, is in the Louvre. It represents Hermes fixing his sandal.

Hermes killing the giant Argos who had eyes all over his body

Aphrodite, Pan and Eros, National Museum of Athens

APHRODITE
(VENUS)

Aphrodite, the most beautiful of the goddesses, was the goddess of love; "she is the one who created desire among gods, human beings, birds of the sky and all wild animals and sea monsters...".

Aphrodite had a close connection with the Phoenician goddess, Astart. If that is so, the Phoenician deity passing through Greece, lost entirely her eastern character and became pure Greek. The second Homeric Hymn to Aphrodite says that the goddess was born at the cost of the island of Cyprus and thus she was often called "Cyprian" (Kypris). According to Hesiod, as it has already been mentioned, Cronus cut down the immortal genitals of his father Uranus and dropped them in the sea. Round the genitals was formed a white foam, (aphros in Greek) and from this foam was born Aphrodite. The blowing winds brought her gently towards Cyprus. The Horai (Hours) accepted her with great pleasure. They dressed her with golden jewelery and brought her to Mt. Olympus. Thus, the goddess was adopted into the Greek pantheon. The Olympians were overwhelmed and speechless by her beauty, and all the male gods wanted to marry her, even Zeus, the father of gods and men; but every time he desired her, Aphrodite provided for him a mortal woman. Finally, Aphrodite became Hephaestus' consort (see chapter on Hephaestus), but she frequently deceived him; first with Ares (Mars) and then with Dionysos (Bacchus), Hermes and Poseidon.

With Ares she begot many offspring. The best known were Eros (Cupid), Harmonia (Harmony), Deimos and Phobos; the last two always accompanied

Eros, Capitoline Museum

59

Aphrodite, Imeros and Pothos

their father Ares during war and in battles.

Very often Aphrodite had erotic affairs with mortals. Well known was her romance with Anchises, the handsome shepherd who used to live on the tops of Mt. Ida (near Troy); the fruit of this union was Aineias.

Even more handsome was Adonis, who looked like a god. One day, as Adonis was hunting, a wild boar attacked him and killed him. Aphrodite ran despe - rately to help him and as she did not we- ar her sandals, a thorn pricked her foot. From the divine blood of the goddess the roses were dyed red, which until then were only white.

Her humble tears for his death created the anemones ..... Great festivities were held in Adonis' honour, in which only women participated.

The stories that follow show the strength of Aphrodite, the goddess who gover- ned the hearts of gods and mortals. Very often, she played strange games and nobody had the power to stop or change her decisions.

One of Aphrodite's victims was beautiful Helen, Menelaus' wife, and queen of Sparta. One of the most famous legends speaks of this relationship. According to

the Iliad, (it is mentioned already on Hera's chapter) Paris, the handsome prince of Troy, was to be the judge of a beauty contest. He was to choose the most beautiful among three queens of Olympus: Athena, goddess of wisdom; Hera, wife of Zeus and Aphrodite, goddess of love. Paris offered the prize, "a golden apple", to Aphrodite, declaring that she was the best! Aphrodite had promised him the most beautiful of all women as companion and this was beautiful Helen, the daughter of Zeus and Leda. So Helen fell in love with Paris and followed him to Troy. Thus, started the expedition of the Greeks against Troy in order to take her back. Aphrodite took part in the Trojan war in defense of her favourite, Paris.

At another famous expedition, the one of the "Argonauts", Aphrodite made princess Medea, the daughter of King Aetes, the King of Colhis, to fall in love with the great hero Jason. Medea helped him to steal the "Golden Fleece" and she came back to Greece with him. Aphrodite made Ariadne, the daughter of King Minos of Crete fall in love with another great hero, Theseus. The beautiful princess helped him to kill the Minotaur and to come out from the

Labyrinth.

Aphrodite caused also another tragedy. Phaidra, the second wife of Theseus, desperately fell in love with her stepchild Hippolytos, son of Theseus and an Amazon. In vain poor Phaidra tried to get rid of this insane love... (for the above stories, see details in the chapters of the heroes).

Finally, a nice legend is the one of Atalanta. The beautiful maiden could run as fast as the wind. Because she disliked marriage, she organized a contest for all the men who wanted to marry her, telling them whoever could run faster, would be her husband.

No one was able to of course, but Aphrodite wanted to help the young hero Melanippos (or Hippomenes in another version). Thus, she gave him three golden apples from the garden of Hesperides. During the foot race every time that Atalanta approached Melanippos, he dropped one by one the golden apples. As she stopped to pick them up, he raced ahead and thus became her husband.

Aphrodite was thought of as the goddess who also protected marriage under the name of "Urania Aphrodite", in opposition to "Aphrodite Pandimos", who protected the satisfaction of the sexual instinct.

As "Pandimos", she protected the prostitutes who were very often her priestesses. The beauty of some of them inspired the great sculptors who often used them as models to pose for the statues of the goddess.

As it has already been mentioned, the worship of the goddess started from the island of Cyprus and from there spread to the whole of Greece. One of the most famous temples of the goddess was the one in Paphos (Cyprus), where great festivals and mystery rites were performed in her honour.

"Young hospital girls, beguiling creatures in wealthy Corinth, You who burn the amber tears of fresh frankincense, Full often soaring upward In your souls to Aphrodite Heavenly Mother of lovers..."

It is said that the great Athenian hero Theseus was the one who first brought her worship to Attica. On Mt. Hymettus was one of her sanctuaries where there was an extraordinary spring and the sacred water cured sterile women.

The most famous sanctuary of Aphrodite was the one of Corinth. There were more than two-hundred priestesses of the goddess, the "Hetairai", famous for their beauty, who offered their services to visitors. The poet Pindar wrote an ode to celebrate them.

Aphrodite and Adonis

The money that people had to pay to enjoy the nights with the Hetairai, were offered to the sanctuary. Another similar sanctuary of Aphrodite was the one at Sicily.

Related to Aphrodite is the term "Hermaphroditism". Hermaphroditos was the son of Hermes and Aphrodite (already discussed in the chapter on Hermes).

We must also refer to the faithful follower of the goddess Eros. According to Hesiod, Eros (Love), "the fairest of the deathless gods", was the primeval power who governed the world before the birth of the Olympians. This indomitable strength, was connected with Aphrodite, who was the goddess of love and through the centuries was represented in Greek mythology as her son. The great sculptors like Praxiteles and Lyssipos represented him as a lovely smiling child, armed with arrows and a bow, and their destination was the heart of any god or mortal.

In art Aphrodite was represented in the early archaic period in the nude, her hands on the breast or the one hand on her breast and the other covering her sex. She was with wide hips (in statuettes of Cyprus). Later on, during the classical period, sometimes she was dressed with a light Ionic tunic and sometimes entirely nude. Usually the goddess was holding an apple (symbol of love), a pigeon or a flower.

Very famous was the statue by Praxiteles, "Aphrodite of Knidos". Another statue of the goddess, work of Phidias, was at Olympia. In many museums round the world are preserved copies, especially from the Roman period, and help us extremely to imagine the beauty and the perfection of the original statues.

A very famous original statue of the goddess is today in the Louvre, known as "Aphrodite of Milos".

Aphrodite and Ares

HEPHAESTOS
(VULCAN)

Hephaestos, the divine blacksmith

According to Homer, Hephaestos was the son of Zeus and Hera, but in Hesiod, he was the child of Hera alone.

He was the god of fire and metals, the divine blacksmith, a peace-loving god, popular on earth as in heaven.

Hephaestos did not have the beauty and grandeur of the other Olympians. He was crippled and deformed, and his own mother, the queen of heavens, did not accept him as her child.

When the baby Hephaestos was born, Hera was so ashamed of his deformity, that she cast him out of Mt. Olympus, down to the sea. The baby was picked up by Thetis, Nereus' daughter, who brought him up with the help of a few other sea-nymphs, and he lived with them for nine years. According to another account, Zeus cast him out, angry with him because during a quarrel, he defended his mother Hera. After falling all day, Hephaestos was kindly received by the Sinties, the natives of the island Lemnos.

Although Hera disliked him, Hephaestos loved and respected his mother. Once, in order to make her confess the secret of his birth, he made a magnificent armchair for her, as a present. When Hera sat down, invisible chains binded her and she could not move for hours. In vain all the gods begged Hephaestos to set her free. Ares, angrily rushed at him, but Hephaestos forced him to retreat, throwing lighted torches at him. Then, Dionysos, the god of wine, succeeded to get him drunk, and at last he let his mother free, with the promise that Zeus would give him as consort the beautiful Aphrodite. (According to another account, his wife was Aglaia, one of the three Graces). His marriage

63

Hephaestos supported by a Seilenos

to Aphrodite however was unsuccessful, as the very beautiful goddess of love was not the type of the faithful wife (see chapters: Aphrodite, Ares).

Hephaestos obeyed his father Zeus and carried out his orders, even when he did not agree with Zeus' decisions.

Thus, he was forced to tie Prometheus* with chains to the rocks of Caucasus until Hercules unchained the prisoner.

In another incident, when the time came for the birth of Athena, Zeus called Hephaestos to strike his divine head with an ax, and this is how the goddess was born.

Finally, Zeus ordered him to create with clay the first woman, Pandora (all gifts), who was given as a gift to Epimetheus (Prometheus' brother) and thus mankind was created.

According to Homer, the workshop of Hephaestos was situated on Mt. Olympus, and it was built by the god himself. In one of Homer's descriptions, Hephaestos was tall and fat, with wide thick-haired chest; but his thin crooked legs could not hold his weight.

Usually he was represented in art with long hair, dressed with a short tunic without sleeves.

His physiognomy was kind, but his look was clever and sly.

As soon as Hephaestos entered his work-shop, he ordered the fires to strengthen, then he put on it the bronze, the silver, the solder, the gold and with his heavy hammer and his pincers he created his masterpieces.

He created for himself golden statues that looked alive. To these mechanical servants the Olympians gave the power to think, to talk, to walk. These were a type of robots used as servants by Hephaestos, always standing next to

him, helping him to walk and ready to receive his orders.

The god created for his father Zeus the "Aegis" (type of shield) and his golden scepter. For Demeter he made the sickle. For Artemis and Apollo he made the arrows; the trident for Poseidon, the golden cup for Dionysos, the god of wine. He also forged the armour of Achilles (the shield was described in detail in the "S" of the Iliad by Homer), and the golden thorax for Hercules.

Even the magnificent palaces of the gods on Mt. Olympus were built by him. Hephaestos was a deity who was close to humans. He taught them the way to achieve magnificent things with the help of fire, and he became the great patron of the craftsmen.

The god had a few amorous affairs. With his union with Kabeiro, Proteas'* daughter, he gave birth to the Kabeiroi (deities of the fire), who were worshipped on a few islands of the Aegean, such as Lemnos and Samothrace.

Another well known son of Hephaestos was Pylios, the great doctor who cured the hero Philoctetes from an awful wound.

Hephaestos' cult was spread all round Greece and was especially strong in Lemnos. He was also highly esteemed in Phrygia, Carea and Lyceia (in Asia Minor).

In Athens he was often worshipped together with Athena, as she was also patroness of fine arts.

The so called "Theseion" in the Athenian Agora was actually a temple, dedicated to Hephaestos. The statue of the god was in the middle of the temple, next to the statue of Athena. The "Hephaestia" was a great procession, and was held every five years in his honor.

---

* Prometheus: He was a Titan, the son of Iapetus and Clemen. He secretly offered fire to the poor humans and for this disobedience he was punished by Zeus.

* Proteas: He was often said to be Poseidon's son. He had the power of foretelling the future and of changing his shape, according to his will.

ARES
(MARS)

Ares, the son of Zeus and Hera, was the most cruel figure of the Greek pantheon. He was the god of War and had but little mythology, as war was not a favourite subject of the Greeks – although they were brave fighters. The gods of Olympus disliked him, and even his father Zeus says – "You are the most odious to me, from all the inhabitants of Olympus because you like always the quarrels, the war and the battles..." Homer calls him "murderous, blood stained, the incarnate curse of mortals..."

During the Trojan War, although he had promised Athena and his mother Hera to help the Greeks, he finally helped the Trojans. Athena then, with Zeus' consent, wore the helmet of Hades (Kini) and became invisible, thus succeeding in helping Diomedes, the great hero, to wound Ares. The god left the battle and went back to Olympus where he was cured by Peon, the doctor of the gods. As already discussed, Ares was the lover of Aphrodite, Hephaestos' wife. Here is a nice story about their illegal love.

The Sun who could see everything, informed Hephaestos about Aphrodite's unfaithfulness. The god unhappy and jealous, thought of a way to take revenge. He created invisible chains, that nobody could untie and spread them on his bed. Then he pretended that he was going to the island of Lemnos for a few days. His plan succeeded and as soon as Ares and Aphrodite lay on the bed, the invisible chains imprisoned them. Hephaestos then appeared and called all the Olympians to see what had happened. The gods laughed at them and as soon as Hephaestos set them free, they ran quickly to hide themselves.

Children of Ares and Aphrodite – if we

Ares, Villa Ludovisi

combine various accounts – were Eros (Love), Anteros (Love Returned), Deimos (Fear), Phobos (Rout) and Harmonia.

A few other offspring of his love affairs are: The nymph Alpina, who gave birth to Inomaos; Althea, who gave birth to Meleagros; Philonome, who gave birth to Lycastos; Pelopeia, who gave birth to Kyknos. Another son of Ares was Diomedes, killed by Hercules, as one of his twelve labours.

Generally, we can say that most of his children resembled him, for they were violent and crafty.

The worship of Ares started from Thrace, which was inhabited by rude and warlike people in the northeast of Greece. Ares did not have many sanctuaries, nor temples to be worshipped in. Pausanias mentions a temple in the ancient Agora of Athens. In the middle of the temple stood the statue of the god, work of the great sculptor Alcamenes. Three other temples of the god are mentioned. One at Troysenia, another at Tegea and the last one near Sparta.

The inseparable followers of Ares were his two sons. Deimos and Phobos (already mentioned); his sister Eris, which means discord, and Strife, her son. Also he is accompanied in battles by the dreadful demons of the war Enyo, (in Latin Bellona), which means terror trembling, Panic and Keres. The last ones were horrible and ghastly, spreading destruction and fear everyone was

Eris (discord), one of the inseparable followers of Ares

afraid of them, according to the description of the poet Apollonius Rhodius. The chariot of Ares was driven by the wild horses, sons of an Eriny.

Symbols of the god were the spear, and the lighted torch. His sacred animals were the dog and the vulture.

Ares killing a giant

Dionysos on a boat trip

DIONYSOS
(BACCHUS)

Dionysos was the god of wine and vine, the god of the happy life and merry-making, but also of agriculture as well as being the patron of the theatre. Probably he was the most popular god of ancient Greeks. The ancient authors and mythologists do not agree with what is said about Dionysos. There are many fantastic stories about his birth and his life, and many opinions about their origins. Some maintain that he came from Phrygia or even India, others that his worship started from Thrace. We are going to accept the most prevalent, that he was born in Thebes in Boeotia. His father was Zeus and his mother a mortal princess of Thebes, Semele, the beautiful daughter of King Cadmus, son of Agenor.

As soon as Hera learned about the new infidelity of her husband, she took revenge. She appeared in front of Semele, transformed as an old lady, and advised her to ask Zeus for a favour, which was to appear in front of Semele in his whole glory and majesty. Poor, credulous Semele forced Zeus to swear by the Styx, the oath that nobody could break that he was going to do everything she wished. In vain Zeus tried to make her change her mind. He was forced by his oath and appeared in front of the poor princess among his lightnings and thunder bolts. Unlucky Semele fell down dead. Then Zeus rescued her unborn child from her body and as there was no time to be born, he put him in his thigh for three months to complete the gestation period. When the time came, the baby Dionysos was born from his father's leg and Zeus asked Hermes to take care of him as he was still afraid of Hera's jealousy. Hermes took the baby

A prancing Maenad wears a snake as headdress and carries a staff and a leopard cub

69

Dionysos, the god of wine and vine

to the Nymphs of Nysa, a place which is unknown to us. The Nymphs accepted to raise him and they became his companions and followers.

In a few days – enough for a god to grow up – Dionysos started to wander in the forests. His head was crowned with a wreath of ivy and vine leaves, and the Nymphs followed him singing and dancing.

According to the seventh Homeric Hymn, which bears his name, one day on the island of Naxos, as Dionysos was walking along the seaside, a Tyrrhenian pirate ship appeared. The pirates thought that Dionysos was a young prince, probably the son of a great King, and so they seized him, hoping for a big ransom and carried him on board ship. They tried then to bind him on the mast of the ship, but in vain the ropes broke immediately and left him free. Then, the helmsman called out: "You fools, don't you see he is a god? Let us put him back on the shore at once, or deadly harm will come to us". But the captain did not agree and thus miracles began to happen. First, the salty water of the sea round the boat became aromatic wine. From the big mast grew a huge vine with branches of grapes, while ivy crawled up like a garland. Then, Dionysos was transformed into a lion and jumped on the captain and the sailors roaring terribly. Terrified they fell into the sea and they were instantly changed into dolphins. The only one who was left, was the good helmsman.

The following is another famous adventure of Dionysos on the island of Naxos. The great Athenian hero Theseus (there is a special chapter on him) killed the Minautaur in the labyrinth of Crete. He succeeded with the help of the princess Ariadne, the beautiful daughter of King Minos, who had fallen in love with him. Theseus promised to take her back to Athens and marry her. On the way back, the boat stopped for a while on the island of Naxos. Ariadne walked round the beautiful island, and as she was tired, she fell asleep at the sea-shore. It was a good chance for Theseus to abandon her and to turn back to Athens without her, but Ariadne had better luck. Dionysos saw her alone sleeping deeply. He fell in love with her and married her. Zeus, to please Dionysos, made her immortal. Three children were born from Ariadne and Dionysos; Inopionas, Evanthes and Staphylos. Their names are connected with the cultivation of the vine.

During the war of the gods against the Giants, Dionysos took part with his attendants: the Seilenoi* and the Satyrs*, who rode on donkeys. The Giants became really terrified when the donkeys started braying!

Wherever Dionysos passed, magnificent and extraordinary things happened. Wine springs appeared from the earth and the rocks. Instead of water the rivers offered milk and honey.

Here is a characterisation of the god by Euripides:

"Dionysos is the god of delight. He reigns in feasts among flower wreaths. He enlivens the joyful dances with the sounds of his flute, he provokes mad laughter and turns away black thoughts. His nectar on the table of the gods increases their happiness and mortals find forgetfulness in his blissful cup of wine".

Dionysos though, persecuted the unbelievers in his divinity. Thus, passing from Thrace, King Lycourgos attacked Dionysos and his nurses. Zeus punished

---

*Seilenoi: They were without number. Their origin was Thrace and Phrygia. These demons were very hairy. They resembled the Centaurus, who had hoofs and legs of horses. Usually they had horses' ears and horses' tails.
*Satyrs: These deities looked like goat-men, with long horns, a tail and hooked nails. They originated in the Peloponnese being spirits of wild life, of woods and mountains and particularly of unrestrained fertility.

him with blindness and he died soon, for he became hateful to the immortal gods. Another king, Pentheus of Thebes, who refused the cult of Dionysos, was torn to pieces by his mother Agave, who was struck with madness by the god (Euripides, Bacchae).

In Argos, says Apollodoros, they would not recognize his divinity, and madness fell upon the daughters of King Proitos, who destroyed their own children. Finally, Melampus, the great doctor healed them.

**Seilenos and the infant Dionysos,
Vatican Museum**

The god was worshipped all round Greece. Typical of the worship of Dionysos was that the faithful went into a delirium – they became possessed. The Dionysian worship had an orgiastic character and very often the festivals held in his honour, ended in orgies, where especially women played a role. The places that the god preferred were the tops of mountains and the best time for his cult was at night.

In the city of Thebes where he was born the god had no sanctuary. The great festival in his honour, the "Trieterica", was held on the slopes of Mt. Cithaeron, during the night, under the light of torches. It was a festival just for women.

The train of women, the Maenads or Bacchantes as they were also called, were crowned with ivy wreaths, their long hair streaming down their shoulders; they were dressed with fawnskins over their robes. They beat drums and danced orgiastically, running like maniacs on the mountain, calling the name of the god and singing:

"O Bacchanals, come,
Oh, come
Sing Dionysos,
Sing to the timbrel
Joyfully praise him,
Him who brings joy..."

Festivals in Dionysos' honour were held in Greece from the beginning of the sixth century B.C. The most brilliant of these were celebrated in Attica. They were divided in two: the Lesser and the Great Dionysia. The Lesser Dionysia had an agricultural character, as the god was also patron of agriculture and fertility. According to Plutarch ".. in front of the procession was a huge amphora (jar), filled with wine and decorated with a branch of vine. Then followed a ram, a basket with figs and last the sacred symbol, a huge phallus".

During the Great Dionysia (called also Urban) they had many ceremonies. The most important was to transfer the cult statue (xoanon) of the god through the city from his temple to another sanctuary. There was a big procession with officials, priests, horsemen, other citizens and maidens from the noble families, carrying baskets with offerings (caniphory). Men disguised as satyrs and Seilenoi were dancing round the statue of the god, while the chorus sang the "Dithyramb" (hymn) in his honor, accompanied by flutes. The procession passed through the Agora of Athens and finally stopped on the southern slopes of the Acropolis in the janctuary of the god where the ancient theater of Dionysos was. This is the oldest theater in the

Dionysos and Ariadne surrounded by Satyrs and Maenads

world and its ruins are preserved to our days. The performances in the theater started with the Dithyramb contests. The greatest poetry in Greece and among the greatest in the world was written for Dionysos.

Later, during the classical period the dramatic contests in the theater lasted four days. They were real competitions with judges and prizes. Thus were born the immortal tragedies by Aeschylus, Sophocles, Euripides and the comedies by Aristophanes.

Other famous sanctuaries of Dionysos were on the islands of Delos, Lemnos, Naxos, Chios, Corfu, Kos, Lesbos, as well as in Pergamon and Egypt.

Animals dedicated to the god were the bull, the goat, the pig, the donkey, the panther, the tiger and the lion.

His sacred plants were the vine, the ivy, the oak-tree, the walnut-tree, the fig-tree, the rose and the asphodel.

His emblems were the "thyrsos" that he used as a weapon and as a magic-stick. At the beginning the thyrsos was a piece of hollow wood with branches. Later on, instead of leaves, it had on its top the cone of a pine-tree, wrapped up with vine-leaves and ivy. When Dionysos touched somebody with the thyrsos, his heart was filled up with enthusiasm that bordered on madness.

In early Greek art, Dionysos was represented as a bearded man. Later on, during the fourth century B.C. he was represented as a handsome youth, usually dressed with skins of goats or panthers carrying a vase (cantharos, rython or skyphos).

Pan, the goat-footed and kind-hearted god

PAN

Pan, Florence

According to the Homeric Hymn, Pan was the son of Hermes and the Nymph Dryope. He was the goat-footed and kind-hearted god of shepherds and flocks. With the passage of time he became also a deity of healing and curer of evils. He knew all the secrets of the forests and of the earth, for he lived close to Mother Earth.

According to the legend, Hermes, on a visit to Arcadia (Peloponnesos), stayed in the forest of Kyllene as a shepherd with his sheep. There he met the Nymph Dryope and fell in love with her. As soon as the Nymph gave birth to their son, her heart was filled with terror. The baby Pan was very unusual. He was shaggy with hair all over, from his waist downwords he was like a goat, with a tail and on his head he had two short horns and goat's ears. The mother abandoned her baby and ran away. Hermes, his beloved father however, when he looked at this clever and happy being, tenderly wrapped the baby in a rabbit's skin and ran up on Mt. Olympus.

There, he presented Pan to the immortal Gods, and they all accepted him with enthusiasm and joy. The one who was more pleased with the strange creature was Dionysos, the god of wine. He called the baby "Pan" which means "All" or "Everybody", because all of them were pleased when they saw him. Thus, Pan was often part of the retinue of Dionysos.

The cult of Pan started from Arcadia the place were he was born, and from there it spread round Greece.

The God loved the green prairies and the high mountains. He liked to walk there the whole day, and he was carefree and happy, followed by the Nymphs. He played his flute sweetly, that even the birds stopped to listen.

His love affairs were fairly numerous. He was fond of all the Nymphs of the mountains, trees, springs and rivers, but was always rejected because of his ugly appearance.

Once, Pan fell in love with lovely Syrinx, one of the Hamadryads (Nymphs of trees). The Nymph, afraid of him, started to run in order to escape. The god ran after her, trying to explain that he only wanted her and meant no harm.

Pan and boy, from a vase painting

Syrinx ran to the shore of Ladon River and begged him to save her. The River-God transformed her into a reed, just the moment that Pan was ready to touch her. Pan full of grief stopped motionless, holding the cane in his hand. Suddenly he got an idea: Cutting off a piece from the cane, he fashioned a musical instrument of seven reeds of different lengths, giving different notes, this was known as "Syrinx" (Pan-pipe).

A second unfortunate love was the Nymph Pitys (Pine). She was loved by both, Pan and Boreas, the wind god. The Nymph preferred Pan, and Boreas got so angry, that he blew such a strong wind, throwing her off a cliff. Then Mother-Earth saw how grieved Pan was and transformed Pitys into the tree that bears her name, the pine.

More tragic was the story of the Nymph Echo. Pan fell in love with her. As she tried to escape running away on the mountains, the god sent madness upon the shepherds, who tore her to pieces, only her voice survived, the echo...

Paniny was the wife of Pan and their children were named Paniskoi. The whole family looked like him; half human half goat with goat's horns.

The cult of Pan according to Herodotos' opinion rapidly spread in Athens in the period of the Persian wars. When the Persian army threatened the city of Athens, the Athenians sent the runner Pheidippides to ask help from Sparta, as the Persian menace did not endanger only Athens, but all of the Greek cities. The Spartans though refused with the pretext that they had a religious celebration and that they would send help with the new moon.

Pheidippides, the runner, coming back to Athens, related to the Athenians that on his way back, he was stopped by Pan near Mt. Parthenion, who asked him sorrowfully why the Athenians did not worship him.

After the great victory of Marathon against the Persians, the Athenians believed that it was Pan who helped them to win. The god raised a çry, spreading "panic" and confusion to the enemies; thus the word panic was born from Pan's terror.

The Athenians, after the battle, took the god into their city and gave him a shrine below the Acropolis, where he was given divine honours.

The main symbols of Pan were Pan's pipe (Syrinx), the flask, the cymbal and the staff with which he slew hares (lagobolon).

His sacred animals were the dog and the rabbit. From the birds he preferred the eagle, as well as the griffin. The plants sacred to him were the ivy and pine-tree.

Great sculptors, like Skopas and Praxiteles, made statues of the god.Great painters, like Mycon and the greatest of them Zeuxis, represented him in magnificent paintings.

ASKLEPIOS
(AESCULAPIUS)

Asklepios was the god of healing, son of Apollo and the mortal Coronis, daughter of Phlegyas. At the beginning he was worshipped as a hero, but there is no doubt that during the historical times he was worshipped as a god elevated to the Olympian ranks and adopted to the Greek Pantheon.

Apollo fell in love with Coronis. The princess though, while she was pregnant expecting Apollo's son, fell in love with a mere mortal, Ischys of Arcadia.

Apollo soon discovered the unfaithfulness of his lover. His bird, a crow with snowy plumage brought him the news. The angry god punished the messenger bird by turning its white plumage into black. Then, he asked Artemis the huntress, his twin sister, to take vengeance on Coronis.

The goddess killed the unfaithful girl, shooting her with one of her golden arrows. Apollo though, did not allow the child of his pregnant lover to be lost. He gave him birth and then decided that the best for his son was to be raised by the Centaur of Magnesia, Cheiron*, and asked him to teach his son the art of medicine.

Asklepios grew up under the supervision of the wise centaur and the pupil surpassed his master in medicine. He became so famous that sick people from all round the ancient world ran to him to be cured, either by the method of using herbs and magical diets, or by surgical

Centaur, Louvre

* Chiron or Cheiron: The centaur Chiron was half human and half horse. He was the son of the Titan Cronus and lived in a cave on Mt. Pelion.
He was the wisest and most fairest of all creatures on earth. All the young heroes used to be brought to him, as he was the only capable to teach them and make them real heroes.

Asklepios, the god of healing, National Museum of Athens

operations.

According to Diodorus Siceliotis*, the god of the underworld, Hades protested to Zeus that Asklepios cured people that were meant to die, or even resurrected them from the dead, as in the case of Hippolytos, Theseus' son. This was disturbing nature's way and universal order. Zeus then struck Asklepios with a thunderbolt and slew him. Later on with Apollo's intervention, Asklepios was deified and went to Mt. Olympus and joined the Greek pantheon.

By his wife (variously named Epione, Ippone, Xanthe, Aglaia) he had many offspring. His two sons, Machaon and Podaleirios became famous; they were the two epic heroes who took part in the Trojan war. Machaon was the one who took out the arrow from Menelaus' wound and cured the awful wound of the hero Filotctetes. The daughters of Asklepios were Hygeia (Health), Panakeia (Cure all) and Iaso (Healing). The most famous was Hygeia, who became the goddess of health, and she was usually worshipped together with her father.

The worship of Asklepios spread all over Greece. The archaeological spade brought to light more than 300 sanctuaries called "Asklepeia". It is worthwhile to report the way that these sanctuaries-sanatoriums functioned. They all were built in idyllic and peaceful places with water springs and rich vegetation. Priest-doctors, the Asclepiadae, as they named the descendants of Asklepios, served the god and maintained the secrets of healing, which were passed from father to son. These priests were scientist-doctors, who had given an oath not to reveal the secrets of their science to the uninitiated.

As soon as the patient arrived at the sanatorium-sanctuary, he first had a

---

Diodorus Siceliotis: (Diodorus of Sicily) Famous Greek historian (90-21 B.C.)

bath "to purify his body". In most of the sanctuaries there was a sacred spring from which the sick drank water "to purify the soul". Then, he was ready to assist at the sacrifices. He sacrificed a cock or a goat, very often a pig, or as it happened in Athens, he burned wheat on the altar. The priests recited the sacred words and prayers, and the attendants repeated them. Now the patient could enter the temple of the god. We must add that on entering the sanatorium-sanctuary, the sick was put on a strict diet. He had to pass the night in the porch which was connected to the temple or in some place adjacent to it. The porch was specially built as a dormitory. There was no light in it and the priests had already prepared the sick for the appearance of the god, which usually took place in his dreams. The god himself would reveal to him how he could be cured.

From the above account we realize today that the power of autosuggestion was understood by these priest-doctors. Through the centuries, though, people stopped being so religious and pious. Procedures were simplified. Instead of the patient sleeping, the priest did so and he was the one to whom Asklepios appeared in his dream and gave istructions for the therapy.

The priest-doctors achieved in time great experience and a medical tradition. It is certain that thousands of people were cured as a result of their scientific methods. They paid great attention to hygiene of the patient. Daily gymnastic exercises were compulsory especially for fat people. Great emphasis was placed on psychology too, trying in every way to understand the patients' psychological problems. This is the reason that various kinds of entertainment, and especially spectacles, theatrical performances and athletic games, were offered to the patients.

We must state that in the sanctuaries of

Asklepios the entrance was forbidden to some people, such as pregnant women and deformed persons. In case the patient died, the priest had the justification that it was God's will not to be cured, so as not to disturb the order of nature.

As soon as the patient recovered, he could leave the sanctuary, but he first had to pay the god some coins or make another type of offering. In most of Asklepios' sanctuaries, archeologists have found hundreds of marble, terracotta or metal offerings, which are in the shape of the cured part of the body; an eye, a nose, an ear, a penis, a hand or a leg. When Christianity replaced the pagan religion, the Christian church adopted this ancient custom. Even now, people that are healed offer to the saint of a church little silver models of their cured member.

The most famous sanctuary of Asklepios was the one of Epidaurus in the Peloponnese. There, in the peaceful green valley on the slopes of Mt. Arachnaeon was built a perfect sanatorium. Epidaurus in our days, offers the visitor the same indescribable calmness that the visitors of the fourth century B.C. must have felt. Magnificent edifices, a glorious theatre* built by Polycleitus, offered the patients the chance to pass their time happily, without cares, hel - ping their own cure.

In the temple of the god stood the gold and ivory statue of Asklepios, the work of Thracymedes.

Another famous Asclepeion was the one of the island of Kos, which was probably the most rich and luxurious, famous especially for its art masterpieces. The great doctor Hippocrates, "the father of medicine", was born on the island of Kos. In our days, the young doctors before starting their practice, are obliged to give the "Hippocratic Oath", showing the great influence that ancient Greek medical tradition carried to our times. Modern medicine once more seeks respectfully to study the methods used by the Greeks some 2.500 years ago.

The Asklepeion of Athens was built on the southern slopes of the Acropolis, near the theater of Dionysos. It was built in 431 B.C., after the great epidemic of the plague when hundreds of Athenians died. It was only then that they felt the necessity of the divine doctor, because until then it was the secondary deities that helped the sick.

Another well known sanctuary of Asklepios was the one in Pergamum. There, another famous doctor of antiquity was born in the second century A.D., – Galinos.

Sacred symbols to Asklepios were the cypress, the pine-tree and the olive-tree. From the animals, the god preferred the dog, the goat, the cock and especially the snake. It is well known that in most of the sanctuaries of the god, the priests used snakes as part of the cure.

The greatest sculptors of antiquity, like Myron, Phidias, Polycleitos, Scopas and Alkamenes carved statues of Asklepios. From the surviving statues, Asklepios is shown as a mature bearded man with long hair. He has a sweet, peaceful and serious expression. He wears a long garment which leaves the chest uncovered. In some statues he holds a stick with a snake curling around it. In some other statues the god is represented with his daughter Hygeia. She appears as a beautiful young lady accompanied by the snake.

---

* Theater of Epidaurus: The surviving theater of Epidaurus, one of the finest in the ancient world, is the best preserved in Greece today. Every summer, the Festival of Epidaurus takes place there.

PART II

HEROES

HEROES

The heroes of Greek mythology were mortals who became deified. They were offspring of marriages between gods and mortals, so they were half-god, half-human.

They lived in the world among mankind and did wonderful and extraordinary deeds. Their guests took them to mysterious lands in order to overcome strange obstacles and fight fierce monsters.

Their bodies died, but their souls lived for ever. Some were even carried into heaven. On their deaths, most of the heroes became demi-gods and protectors, and guardians of the cities where they were buried. Their worship was similar in many ways to the medieval veneration of the saints of the Christian church.

In the second part of this booklet are mentioned the most famous and prominent heroes of Greek mythology.

HERACLES, THESEUS, PERSEUS, JASON, BELLEREPHON, DAEDALUS AND ICARUS, PHAETHON, ORPHEUS and a name list of HEROES OF THE TROJAN WAR.

HERACLES
(HERCULES)

Farnese Hercules, Naples Museum

He was the son of Zeus and Alkmene, wife of Amphitryon. Zeus fell in love with Alkmene and one day when Amphitryon was away fighting, Zeus took Amphitryon's form and visited her. From this union issued the greatest hero, the mightiest of mortals of the ancient world, Heracles. The same night, the real Amphitryon came to Alkmene and so she bore two children, Heracles to Zeus and Iphicles to Amphitryon.

Hera, as always jealous, became furious and to take revenge, she sent two serpents to attack Heracles in his cradle. The newborn Heracles though, clut - ched the throats of the serpents in his hands and strangled them to death. Great care was taken with his education. The best masters taught him fen - cing, boxing, wrestling, fighting in armour and driving the chariot. Thus he grew up and when he was eighteen, he killed the great lion of Mt. Cithaeron. After this, he fought against the Minyans, the neighbouring city which had held Thebes under tribute and set it free. Grateful, the King of Thebes Creon, gave him as reward his daughter Megara in marriage. Megara bore him three sons. Hera, who always perse- cuted Heracles, sent a madness upon him and he killed Megara and his chil- dren. Recovering his mind, he needed to be purified. He sought out the Delphic oracle and he was told that by Zeus' order he must serve his cousin Eurys- theus, the king of Tiryns and Mycenae. According to Apollodorus, Heracles accepted the Delphic oracle, ready to do anything that could make him clean again. The twelve impossible tasks Eurystheus gave him to do are called: "the Labours of Heracles".

The First Labour was to kill the Nemean Lion, the offspring of Orthos and Echidna, or son of the monster Typhon. As the lion could not be wounded by iron or other metal, Heracles choked it in his hands. Then he wore the skin and this is the way that artists usually represented him.

The Second Labour was to kill the Lernean Hydra, meaning "water snake", the offspring of Typhon and Echidna. The monster which lived in a swamp, had nine heads. When Heracles chopped off one head, two grew in its place. A hero then, called Iolaos, his nephew, came for help. Whenever Heracles cut off a head, Iolaos burnt the stump, so that new ones could not grow.

The Third Labour involved the Hind of Keryneia, the sacred deer of Artemis with the golden antlers and the brazen feet. Heracles chased it for a whole year before he succeeded in its capture.

The Fourth Labour was to catch the Erymanthian Boar. Heracles chased him untill the boar fell exhausted and the hero brought it alive to Eurystheus.

The Fifth Labour was to clean the Augean Stables in a single day. Augeias, the son of Helius, was the King of Elis. The stables had thirty thousand cattle and had never been cleaned! Heracles succeeded by turning the course of the river Alpheios through the stables.

The Sixth Labour was to kill the Stymphalian Birds. These birds had brazen claws, wings and beaks, and lived around the lake of Stymphalos in Arcadia. Goddess Athena gave Heracles a bronze rattle with which the hero made a great noise. The birds afraid came out of their covers and as they flew up, Heracles shot them.

The Seventh Labour had to do with the Cretan Bull. The wild animal belonged to Minos, the King of Crete. Heracles caught it alive, showed it to Eurystheus and then let it free until it reached the plain of Marathon.

The Eighth Labour was about the Horses of Diomedes. He was the savage King of Thrace, the son of Ares and Kyrene. Diomedes fed his wild horses with human flesh. Heracles called for volunteers to help him and attacked Diomedes. The King was killed in a battle and then was fed to his own steeds. This made them tame and Hera-

Heracles killing the Nemean lion

Heracles and Iolaos killing the Lernean Hydra

cles brought them first to Eurystheus and then to Argos, where they were dedicated to the goddess Hera.

The Ninth Labour involved the Girdle of Queen Hippolyte, the queen of the Amazons. The Amazons were a tribe of women who fought on horseback and lived away from the borders of the known world, in Asia Minor. In a battle, the Amazons were defeated, their Queen killed and Heracles brought the girdle to Eurystheus.

The Tenth Labour was to bring back the Oxen of Geryones. Geryones was a monster with three bodies and lived on the island of Erythia at the end of the Mediterranean sea, near the coast of Spain. Heracles arrived at the Straits of Gibraltar and there he set up two pillars, one on each side, which since then have been called "the Pillars of Heracles". The hero then killed Orthos, the two-headed dog and then Geryones himself and drove the cattle back by land to Eurystheus.

The Eleventh Labour was to bring back the golden apples of Hesperides, the daughters of the Titan Atlas, who bore the heavens upon his shoulders. Heracles got Atlas to pluck the apples for

him, while he himself held up the sky. When Atlas came back with the apples, happy with his freedom, he told Heracles he could keep on holding up the sky. The hero was disturbed for a moment and suddenly got the idea! He asked the Titan to hold the sky for just a minute, as he was not used to this weight and he wanted to make a pad for his head. Atlas did so and Heracles picked up the apples and went off to Eurystheus.

The Twelfth Labour was to bring the dog Cerberos, the three-headed dog up from Hades. Heracles succeeded in seizing the dog and carrying him up to earth. He showed him to Eurystheus and then took him back again to the underworld.

Along with these glorious deeds, there were many others. Heracles took part in the battle of the Giants helping the gods. He killed the cruel Giant Antaeus. He joined the quest of the Golden Fleece. He took part in the hunt of the Calydonian boar. He marched with the other famous heroes against Troy. He brought back from the underworld Alkestes, the wife of his friend Admetus.

Finally, he fell in love and married with

Heracles and Cerberos

the princess Deianeira, daughter of Oineus of Calydon. One day, Heracles and Deianeira reached the river Evinos where the Centaur Nessus acted as ferryman. The Centaur attempted to violate Deianeira and Heracles slew him. But before the Centaur died, he advised Deianeira to take some of his blood and keep it safely as a magic erotic filter.

According to Apollodorus, Heracles fell in love with Iole, daughter of Eurytos, King of Oichalia. The King though, refused to give her as wife, and Heracles in a fit of madness killed his son Iphitus. The hero once more visited the Delphic Oracle for advice but the priestess would give him no answer. The hero got angry again and seized Apollo's sacred tripod where the priestess used to sit and left in order to found an oracle for himself. There was a fight between Heracles and Apollo, but Zeus, their father, came between them, dropping one of his thunderbolts. Apollo took back his tripod and Heracles got his answer: to be sold as slave to Omphale, the queen of Lydia and to serve her for three (or one) years. When the years

were up, Heracles was free from his guilt and was ready to come back again. Deianeira, his devoted wife, was meanwhile waiting for him. She heard of his love for Iole and to win him back, she tried the Centaur's poisonous filter. She smeared it on a robe of the hero and sent it to him by a messenger.

When Heracles put on the robe, a fearful pain seized him and his flesh became inflamed. The hero felt that his end was near. The tragic moments of his sacrifice were described by Sophocles in his tragedy, "the Trachinian Women".

Heracles ascended the peak of Mt. Oeta and there he built a great pyre and sat on it. The mortal parts of him were burnt away, the rest ascended to Olympus where he was deified. He was reconciled with Hera and married her daughter Hebe, the goddess of youth.

Heracles was worshipped all over Greece. The festivals and athletic games in his honour were called "Heracleia".

Great sculptors like Lyssipos and Praxiteles created statues of the hero. Many of them, either original Greek or Roman copies, are preserved in many museums round the world.

THESEUS

Theseus was a great Athenian hero, son of Aegeus, King of Athens, and the princess Aethra, daughter of Pittheus, the King of Troezen.

Theseus grew up in the palace of his grandfther in Troezen (N.E. of Argolis in Peloponnese). When he became sixteen years of age, he was strong, brave, wise and intelligent. His mother then took him to a heavy rock and asked him if he could lift it. Theseus moved it easily and under the rock he found the weapons and a pair of sandals that his father had hidden before he left.

Now, the hero knew that his father was King Aegeus, the King of Athens, and decided to make the long trip to Athens to meet him. He went by land although he knew that the journey was dange rous, but the hero did not like the ea sy voyage by ship.

Near Epidaurus, he met and conquered the brigand Periphetes. Near Corinth he met the cruel giant Pityocamptis (Pine-bender), who pulled down two trees, tied to the unfortunate travellers and then let the trees go to tear the people in half. Theseus inflicted on him the same death.

After the Canal of Corinth, he killed Sciron, who used to make travellers kneel to wash his feet and then kicked them over the cliff down into the sea. This place was called since then "the Scironides Rocks".

Near Megara, he met and killed the brigand Procrustes (the Hammerer or Stretcher). This one used to tie his victims on a bed and he either streched those who were short or cut off the legs of those that were longer than the bed. Finally, Theseus destroyed Phae, a

Amazon after Polycleitos,
Berlin Museum

87

dreadful monster and thus the road to Athens was free of these dangers. His fame reached Athens before him. He was already an acknowledged hero. Arriving in Athens he was welcomed by his father King Aegeus, but not by his wife Medea, who tried to poison him. Aegeus who recognized Theseus by his own sword dropped the cup with the poison, thus saving his son's life.

Theseus in Athens fought Pallas and his fifty sons who were his father's enemies. He caught the wild Marathonian bull which had been brought from Crete to Attica by Heracles and sacrificed it to Apollo.

The greatest of his labours was killing the Minotaur, the offspring of Pasiphae, the wife of Minos, and the bull of Poseidon.

The Athenians had been obliged to send seven youths and seven maidens to Crete as tribute for the death of Androgeus, Minos' son. The youths and the maidens were put in the labyrinth where the monstrous half-human, half-bull Minotaur lived to be eaten by him. Theseus killed the monster and saved his compatriots' lives. He was helped by Ariadne, the daughter of Minos, who fell in love with him. She gave him a spool of thread and so Theseus found his way out of the endless twisting corridors of the Labyrinth.

It has already been discussed that on his way back the hero abandoned Ariadne on the island of Dia (Naxos). Arriving in Athens, Theseus forgot to change the

Theseus and the Minotaur

The labours of Theseus

black sails of his boat to white ones, as he had promised his father before star - ting on the voyage. When Aegeus saw the black sails, he thought that his son was killed and so he threw himself into the sea, which since then has been called "The Aegean Sea".

Theseus became King of Athens and he did great things for his city. For the first time the twelve small communities of Attica were united into a great city; the city of Athens, which became the most glorious in the ancient world. He established the great festival of the "Panathenaea" (described in the chapter of Athena). This most wise king made the first laws and most important he established a commonwealth building, a council hall, where citizens for the first time in the world's history could gather and vote.

Theseus received Oedipus, the tragic King of Thebes and offered him hospi-

tality; he sheltered Heracles after the killing of Megara and their children; he took part in the Hunt of the Calydonian boar; he also joined the expedition of the Argonauts to find the Golden Fleece.

Once Theseus was invited by his dear friend Pirithous, the King of the Lapiths, to participate in the big feast of his wedding. The Centaurs (half-horse, half-man) were invited as well, got drunk during the feast and seized the Lapith women. A terrible battle followed where finally the Lapiths with the help of Theseus drove the Centaurs out of their country.

Finally, Theseus fought against the Amazons who were defeated and their queen Antiope (or Hippolyte) became his wife. She gave him a son, Hippolytus, who became the hero of a tragic story. When Antiope died, Theseus married Phaedra, Ariadne's sister. From this second marriage he had two sons, Acamas and Demophon.

His first son, Hippolytus, became a charming youth, great athlete and hunter. Phaedra fell in love with her stepson, a mad and guilty love that Hippolytus repulsed and which brought on his death. The story was described in the tragedy of "Hippolytus" by Euripides.

It is said that the Athenians banished Theseus and the hero went into exile on the island of Scyros at the court of King Lycomedes. There, either he died by accident, or Lycomedes himself murdered him. The Athenians after his death honored him as a demi-god. They brought his relics back to Athens and they built a great tomb in his memory which became a sanctuary for slaves and helpless people. Great festivals were held in his honour, the "Theseia" and the "Epitaphie".

In art, sculptors and vase painters represented him performing his labours. The so-called "Theseion" near the Athenian Agora, which was a temple to Hephaestos, had its friezes decorated with Theseus' tasks.

The great writers, Ovid, Apollodorus and Euripides, gave in detail the life and the labours of this hero, who did good to mankind.

Theseus and Sinis

PERSEUS

Perseus was the son of Zeus and Danae, daughter of the King of Argos Akrisius. This King was afraid of the prophecy that his grand-son would take away his kingdom. He did not want to kill his daughter though, and so he shut her up in an underground bronze chamber. There was only a small part of the room open to the sky, so no one could come near Danae. But Zeus, who could see everything, saw the beautiful maiden in her prison and fell in love with her. He visited Danae in the form of a gold shower, which entered from the small opening of the roof. Thus, Perseus, the son of Zeus was born.

When Akrisius discovered the baby, being afraid of murdering him and his daughter, put them in a wooden box and let them out to sea. The floating box reached the small island of Seriphos, where Polydectes reigned.

Danae was found by Dictys, Polydectes' brother. He was a nice and kind man and took her and her baby in his house. There, Perseus grew up and became a brave, strong and handsome youth. Meanwhile, King Polydectes fell in love with beautiful Danae, but she refused his affection. The king finding that Perseus was an obstacle to his plans decided to get rid of him. So, he asked Perseus to undertake a dangerous adventure; to bring him the head of the Gorgon Medusa!

The gods, though, were watching over Perseus and two of them, Athena and Hermes, came to his aid. They first gave him Hades' helmet, which made him invisible. Then, Hermes lent him his winged shoes of swiftness and a sharp

**Perseus and Andromeda,
Capitoline Museum**

91

Akrisius puts Danae and the baby Perseus in a wooden box.

sword to cut off Medusa's head. He finally gave him a type of sack, in which to put his booty. Next, Athena advised him to fly away to the West, in the land of darkness until he met the three Graiai (Old Hags). They were the only ones who knew the way to the Gorgons. The three Old Hags had only one eye and one tooth among them, which they lent to each other. Their names were Buzzer, Terror and Fury. Perseus stole their one eye and forced them to show him the way. When finally Perseus reached the land where the Gorgons lived, he saw three of them. The Strong and the Leaper, who were immortal, and Medusa, who was mortal. He found her asleep. Athena appeared again and advised him to cut off Medusa's head by looking at her image reflected in his shield, as her awful sight could turn him into a stone.

Thus, the hero cut off the dreadful head, which had snakes instead of hair and dropped it without looking at it, in his sack. From the drops of blood that fell from Medusa's neck sprang Pegassus, the winged horse.

On the way back, Perseus passed through Ethiopia. There, he slew a dragon sent by Poseidon to devour princess Andromeda, daughter of Cassiopeia and Cepheus, King of the Ethiopians. Perseus fell in love with her and made Andromeda his wife.

Together they reached Seriphos and there Perseus was informed that his mother had taken refuge in a temple, because she refused to marry King Polydectes. The hero met the king in his palace and showed him and his supporters, the head of Medusa, at which sight they were all immediately turned into stone.

Perseus made Dictys king of the island and he with his wife and mother went back to Argos. There, he took part in an athletic game, accidentally killing his grand-father, Akrisius, with the discus that he threw, thus fulfilling the prophecy of the Delphic Oracle.

The hero refused the throne of Argos; he took Tiryns in exchange and founded Mycenae. According to one version, he retired to Asia and his son Perses became the ruler of a country which was called after his name, Persia, and became the ancestor of the Persian race. After his death, Perseus was placed in heavens among the constellations.

JASON

This great hero was the son of Aeson, the King of Iolkos in Thessaly. King Aeson was overthrown by his brother Pelias and so Jason was raised by the Centaur Chiron, the most just and wise Centaur, who trained, all the great heroes.

When Jason was grown up, he decided to go back and become King of Iolkos. On the road to the city, he reached a swollen river and met an old woman who was afraid to cross it. The noble hero carried her over on his shoulders but he lost one of his sandals in the water. The old woman he had carried, appeared to him with her real face; she was the goddess Hera, who since then favored him.

When he arrived in Iolkos, his uncle Pelias remembered the oracle that had been foretold of being unthroned by a man wearing one sandal. To get rid of him he swore to restore the throne to him if he would bring back the "Golden Fleece"* from the far away Colchis, where King Aeetes reigned.

Jason knew that the voyage to the unknown far end of the Black Sea was a very dangerous task. It was very important to build a ship which could resist the wind and the storms. Thus, was built the

* "Golden Fleece": A ram with golden fleece was born from the union of Poseidon and Themisto, daughter of Bizaltes. This golden ram was sent by Nephele, the wife of Athamas, to save her children Helle and Phrixus, because their father Athamas was forced by his second wife Ino, to sacrifice them to the gods. The ram with the golden fleece arrived just in time to save them and carried away the children on his back. On the way, Helle fell into the sea, which since then has been called "Hellespont". The ram continued with Phrixus and left him at Kolchis, where King Aeetes gave him his daughter Chalciope as wife.

The fifty-oared Argo was built with Athena's help

fifty-oared "Argo", named after Argos, who built it under Athena's help with pines of Mt. Pelion. Athena herself brought a beam of oak from the oracle of Dodona, which had the power of speech and set it up as the stem.

All famous heroes from Greek cities came to join Jason and participated in the great adventure; this fantastic crew were named the Argonauts. Here is a list of names of few of the participants: Heracles, Castor and Pollux, sons of Zeus; Orpheus, the divine musician; Peleus, Achilles' father; Telamon, father of the Greater Aias; the seers Amphiaraos and Mopsus; Zetes and Calais, sons of the North Wind; Echion, Eurypus and Aethalides, all sons of Hermes; Angaeus and Euphemus, the sons of Poseidon; the heroes Meleagros, Laokoon and Iphiklos that took part also in the "Hunt of the Kalydonian boar" and many others.

They embarked at Pagasae, the port of Iolkos, first reaching the island of Lemnos, inhabited only by women. The Lemnian woman had risen up against the men and all the men were killed. The queen Hypsipyle and the women welcomed the Argonauts and the queen chose Jason as her lover and bore him two sons, Euneas and Thoas.

After they left Lemnos where they passed a year, they entered the Hellespont and landed at Kios. There Hylas, the son of Theiodamas and the dear friend of Heracles went to search for water; but he was bewitched by the nymph of a spring and disappeared. Heracles set out searching for him and finally Argo had to sail without them.

Next stop was the country of Bebrykes, where Amycus, the son of Poseidon reigned. The king was very inhospitable and killed in boxing matches, all strangers who reached his country. Polydeuces (Pollux) though was a better boxer and killed Amycus.

Then, they reached Salmydessos,

where they met the old blind man Phineus, who had the gift of prophecy by Apollo. The poor man was trembling from weakness and he was starving as the Harpies seized and befouled his food. The two winged sons of the North Wind, Zetes and Calais, chased the frightful flying Harpies away, liberating Phineus. The blind prophet, thankful, advised the Argonauts how to sail through the two clashing rocks – the "Symplegades" that closed together and then moved apart – at the entrance of the Black Sea.

Jason followed his advice and sent a dove before them. The bird flew among the Clashing Rocks with only its tail-feathers being cut off. Quickly they rowed with all their strength and passed through the rocks with only a little damage at the extreme end of Argo's stern. Since then the rocks have remained separated, never having moved again. The ship reached now the southern shore of Pontus, where the King of the Maryandini, Lycus, accepted them kindly. There, they went on a hunting trip where one of the heroes, the seer Idmon, was killed by a wild boar.

Next stop was the island of the god Ares, where the Argonauts were attacked by the Stymphalian birds, which Heracles had forced to leave their birth-place, the Stymphalian Lake. They got rid of them following Heracles' plan making a great noise by striking their swords with their shields. The birds with the brazen beaks and brazen feathers were frightened and flew far away.

The Argo now reached the land of Colhis, the country of the Golden Fleece. They went to the palace of Aeetes and Jason asked him for the fleece. The king answered that he would give it to him only if he would first put a yoke on the bronze bulls of Hephaestus which breathed fire out of their mouths, and then plough a field; next he had to sow the field with the teeth of Cadmus' dra-

Goddess Athena, Jason and the dragon

gon* and then destroy the armed men who sprang from the dragon's teeth. The tasks seemed impossible, but Jason could not refuse.

Meanwhile at Olympus, Hera and Athena both favouring Jason, asked for Aphrodite's help. She sent her little son Cupid (Eros) and caused the daughter of Aeetes, Medea, to fall in love with Jason. Medea was an echantress, a priestess of Hecate*, "the goddess of ghosts". She provided Jason with a magic ointment and advised him to anoint his body with it. This charm was called the "root of Prometheus" and could make him proof against fire for one day. Jason succeeded in putting a yoke on the bulls, he ploughed and

Jason putting a yoke on the bull

sowed the field and when the armed men grew from the dragons' teeth, he threw a great stone among them. The men rushed together fighting and killed each other.

Medea showed Jason the oak tree from which the fleece hung. A dragon which never slept guarded the tree and nobody could approach. Medea charmed the dragon who fell asleep and Jason took the fleece down.

Jason took Medea with him on the long retun journey. Some say that they sailed up the river Danube (Ister), passing down into the Rhone, then into the Rhine and into the Ocean Stream. They arrived at the Straits of Gibraltar and so they reached the Mediterranean sea. They passed from Aiaie, Kirkes' island, they reached the dangerous pass between Skylla and Charybdis. They arrived at the island of Sirens and they were saved from hearing their song by Orpheus who played on his lyre. At the shores of Libya they had to carry Argo overland on their shoulders for twelve days and nights, until they came to lake Tritonis, and from there they reached the sea again. They passed from Crete where Medea saved them from Talos, the bronze giant who guarded the island by walking round it three times a day. Finally, they returned to Iolkos. King Pelias was an old man now. Medea advised his daughters to restore their fathers' youth with a charm. So, they boiled Pelias in a couldron with Medea's magic herbs which caused his death.

After Pelias' death, his son Akastos, drove Medea and Jason out of the country and they went to Corinth. Jason fell in love and married Glauke, the daughter of Creon, the King of Corinth. The cruel revenge of Medea is described in Euripides' great tragedy "Medea". She murdered their two children, Mermeros and Pheres, and then escaped stepping into a chariot drawn by winged dragons. She arrived in Athens and married the old King Aegeus, Theseus' father.

Jason took his own life out of despair at the loss of his children. According to another version though, he was killed by a piece of wood coming loose from his ship Argo and falling upon him.

BELLEREPHON

Bellerephon and Pegasus

He was son of Glaucus, king of Corinth and Eurynome. Bellerephon (or Bellerephontes in Homer) murdered unwillingly his brother and went to Argos, where he was purified by King Proetus. Queen Anteia, the wife of Proetus, fell in love with the young hero and to take revenge because he refused her love, falsely accused him to the king. Proetus expelled Bellerephon and sent him to Iobates, ,the king of Lycia in Asia. He also asked the hero to take a letter to Iobates; Bellerephon accepted without knowing that the message in the letter was to put him to death immediately.

King Iobates received the hero with rich hospitality. Instead of slaying him, he commanded him to perform certain heroic deeds, assured that he would never succeed. He asked him to slay Chimaera, a monster with a lion's head, a goat's body and a long snake for a tail. Smoke came out of his mouth and he had an awful smell. Chimaera did great damage by killing people or destroying their crops. Bellerephon accepted as the king also promised to give him his beautiful daughter in marriage if the hero was successful.

He first went back to Corinth and slept outside the temple of Athena. The goddess appeared to him in his dream and gave him a golden bridle, the first ever seen. The hero woke up and went to the famous spring Pirene. Then, he saw Pegasus, the winged horse coming down through the sky to drink of the sweet water. He put the golden bridle round Pegasus' neck and together they flew back to Lycia. He found the place where Chimaera was and succeeded in slaying the monster.

Then, King Iobates asked him to go on an expedition against the Solymi, a tribe of warriors. The hero succeeded again and conquered them.

The third task was to do battle against the Amazons. When Bellerephon came back victorious, Iobates realized that the hero was not a common mortal. Despaired of killing him, he gave him his daughter Philonoe as his bride, as well as half of his kingdom.

However, the end of Bellerephon's life was tragic, because of insolance. He tried to ride Pegasus up to Olympus to take a place among the gods. On the way up, Pegasus threw the hero to the earth as a punishment by Zeus. He was not killed but remained lame for the rest of his life.

Bellerophon, the King Proetus and the Queen Anteia.

DAEDALUS and ICARUS

Daedalus was the son of Metion (Knowledgeable man) who was a descendant of the craftsman god, Hephaestos. He lived in Athens, but he was exiled because of a murder and so he took refuge in Crete in the court of King Minos. The king received him very gladly, as he knew that Daedalus was a great architect, artist and inventor. As a sculptor, Daedalus became famous, as he was the first who carved his wooden statues (xoana) with the left foot forward, thus giving them a motion – as the old technique was with the feet close together and motionless.

King Minos asked him to build the Labyrinth for the Minotaur and the genius architect built it so complicated that nobody going into it could find his way out.

When the king learned that Daedalus showed the princess Ariadne the way to save Theseus from the Labyrinth, (see chapter on Theseus) he imprisoned Daedalus and Icarus in it.

Icarus was the son of Daedalus and Nausicrates. The youth helped his father to make two pairs of wings; a small for him, a larger for Daedalus and they attached them with wax on their shoulders. They flew like birds away from Crete. Crazy with joy at his freedom and the pleasure of flight, Icarus forgot his father's advice not to go too near the sun. Higher and higher he flew and the sun melted the wax and the wings came off and he dropped into the sea and drowned. Since then this sea has been called "Icarian".

Daedalus, inconsolable with grief, landed at the island of Kyme. He built there a temple to Apollo and dedicated his

Daedalus and Icarus making the pairs of wings

wings to the god. From there, he went to Sicily, where he was kindly received by King Cocalus.

Meanwhile, King Minos was in a great fury because of this unbelieveable escape, and searched round the world for Daedalus. Wherever he passed, he put a puzzle to people he met. He knew that only Daedalus would be able to find the answer. "If anyone could pass a thread through a shell twisted round and round..." he would be given a rich reward by the king!

Finally, he arrived in Sicily and put the puzzle to King Cocalus. The king asked Daedalus who easily solved the problem. He took an ant and tied it with a thread. The ant entered the shell and went round and round the spirals, coming out of the other side, passing the thread along with it. Minos realized that Daedalus was nearby. King Cocalus though, refused to deliver him. Finally, Minos was drowned in his bath by the three daughters of Cocalus.

The Fall of Icarus P. P. Rubens (1577-1640),
Musées Royaux des Beaux - Arts de Belgique in Brussels.

PHAETHON

Phaethon (Shiner) was the son of Helius (Sun)*, and the Oceanid Clymene. When he grew older, he asked his mother about his father. Clymene assured him that his father was the Sun-god and that it was time to meet him.

Phaethon reached the far East where his father's place was. When they met, his father, in order to please him, promised to grant him any wish.
Phaethon begged Helios to allow him to drive the divine chariot with the marvellous horses round the world for just one day. In vain Helios tried to change his son's mind. Phaethon was not concerned with dangers and had made his choice...
The promise was kept and Helios gave him some last advice. The four divine horses, Fiery, Shiny, Scorcher and Blazer harnessed to the chariot started on the daily race.
Soon they felt that they were not driven by the usual charioteer but by unskilled hands and they started a mad race. Phaethon lost control and the chariot came so close to the earth that it set the earth on fire. The forests were burned, the waters came to the boiling point, people of Africa especially were burnt black. In order to avoid universal destruction, father Zeus slew Phaethon with a thunderbolt and stopped the mad drive of the chariot.
The body of Phaethon fell into the river Eridanus. His sisters, the Heliades (daughters of Helius), came to mourn for him. They wept for so long till they turned into poplar trees and their tears

Helius (sun)

* Helius (Sun): The son of the Titan Hyperion and the Titaness Theia. He was the personification of the sun and light.

became drops of amber.........
Phaethon's dear friend Kyknos (Swan)
in grief for him turned into a swan.

The Fall of Phaëthon P. P. Rubens (1577-1640),
Musées Royaux des Beaux - Arts de Belgique in Brussels.

ORPHEUS

Orpheus was the son of the Muse Calliope and Oeagros, the King of Thrace (or according to another version, son of Apollo).

It was said that Orpheus was such a marvelous player of the lyre, that his music stopped the course of the rivers; the rocks rolled out of their place following him on his way; the wild beasts on Mount Olympus lay down around him to listen!

He was one of heroes of the Argonaut expedition. It has been mentioned (see chapter on Jason) that he saved the Argonauts from the magic music of the Sirens by playing his own lyre. According to one version, he and not Medea, put the sleepless dragon who guarded the golden fleece to sleep with his divine music.

Orpheus married Eurydice whom he loved very much, but, their happiness lasted briefly. Eurydice trod on a snake and died from its poisonous bite.

Desolated, he determined to go down to the world of Death, to bring her back again! The sound of his lyre enchanted Cerberos, the three-headed dog and let him pass through the gate to the dark Kingdom of the underworld. He met King Hades and queen Persephone and the three judges of the dead, Minos, Rhadamanthys and Aiacos and asked them to allow him to take Eurydice back to life.

He played his lyre so divinely that no one could refuse him. Eurydice was permitted to follow him, but on the condition that Orpheus should not look back at her until they reached the world of the

Hermes, Eurydice and Orpheus, Villa Albani

living. He could not resist; not hearing her footsteps behind him, he turned his head and Eurydice disappeared for ever slipping back into darkness.

He returned alone to earth desolated and became a lonely man. He founded a mystical religion known as Orphism. The initiated to the mysteries and the ceremonies of purification could gain eternity and immortality of the soul.

His tragic end was during a Dionysian orgy when the Maenads of Thrace fell upon him and tore him to pieces. They cut off his head and flung it into the river Hebros. The head floated out to the sea and came ashore at Methymna (Lesvos). It was found by the Muses who buried it in a sanctuary on the island. His divine lyre was turned into a constellation.

Death of Orpheus, from a vase painting

THE TROJAN WAR

The Trojan War is a historical event and not a fiction of the great poet Homer.
This fact which has been proven by excavations led by the German archaeologist
Henrick Schliemann (1870-1890) caused a great agitation at the time, since it
dispelled the myth and changed the whole theory of historians and archaeologists.
Later on, it was confirmed by the new finds that came to light in many Greek
Mycenean centres.
According to legend, the Greeks carried out the great expedition against Troy, in
order to take back the beautiful Helen of Sparta, abducted by Paris of Troy.
Today it is believed that it was organized by the Greeks, in order to extend their
colonies over the fertile territories of Asia Minor, particularly rich in gold.

Achilles tending the wounded Patroclus

THE HEROES OF THE TROJAN WAR

Here is a list with the most famous heroes of the Iliad

GREEKS (Achaeans)

AGAMEMNON

The King of Mycenae and the supreme leader of the expedition. He was son of Atreus and husband of Clytemnestra, daughter of Tyndareus.

MENELAUS

Son of Atreus and Agamemnon's brother. He was the King of Sparta and husband of beautiful Helen, the daughter of Zeus and Leda.

ACHILLES (Achileus)

The most famous of Greek heroes. Son of the nereid Thetis and Peleus, the King of Phthia; he was the leader of Myrmidones.

AIAS THE GREATER (AJAX THE TELAMONIAN)

The son of Telemon and King of Salamis

AIAS THE LESSER (AJAX THE LOCRIAN)

The son of Oileus and leader of the Locrians. The greatest hero after Achilles.

ODYSSEUS

The King of Ithaka, son of Laertes and Anticlea. He was the husband of Penelope and father of Telemachus.

NESTOR

The old wise King of Pylos, the son of Neleus and Chloris.

DIOMEDES

Son of Tydeus, King of Aitolia and Deipyles, daughter of Adrastos, King of Argos.

PATROKLUS (Patrokles)

The favorite retainer of Achilles.

NEOPTOLEMUS

Son of Achilles and Deidameia, daughter of Lycomedes, King of Skyros.

PALAMEDES

Son of Nauplios and Klymene

IDOMENEUS

The grandson of Minos. He was the King and the leader of Cretans

Achilles and Ajax playing a game

THE TROJANS
and their Allies

PRIAM

The King of Troy, the son of Laomedon. He had fifty sons by various wives. His chief wife was Hecabe (Hecuba), the daughter of Dymas, King of Phrygia.

HECTOR

Son of King Priam and Hecave. He was the husband of Andromache, daughter of Aetion, King of Thebes in the Troad. He was the most celebrated of the Trojan heroes.

PARIS
(Alexander)

The younger son of King Priam and Hecave. He abducted Helen and caused the Trojan war.

AENEAS

Son of the shepherd Anchises and goddess Aphrodite.

CASSANDRA
(or Alexandra)

Daughter of Priam and Hecabe. She had the gift of prophecy, but she was never believed.

LAOCOON

Priest of Apollo in Troy. Son of Antinor and husband of Antiop.

SARPEDON

Son of Zeus and Europa, the leader of the Lycians.

RHESUS

Son of one of the muses, the leader of the Thracians.

MEMNON

Son of Eos and Tithonos, the dark-skinned leader of the Ethiopians.

PENTHESILEIA

Daughter of Ares, the queen of the Amazons.

The contest of the Lapiths and the Centaurs, from the Parthenon.